Amazing Missionary Adventures

What is it really like to be a missionary

by Ronald F. Peters

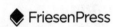

FriesenPress

One Printers Way
Altona, MB R0G 0B0
Canada

www.friesenpress.com

Copyright © 2023 by Ronald F. Peters
First Edition — 2023

ISBN
978-1-03-916628-8 (Hardcover)
978-1-03-916627-1 (Paperback)
978-1-03-916629-5 (eBook)

1. RELIGION, CHRISTIAN LIFE, PERSONAL MEMOIRS

Distributed to the trade by The Ingram Book Company

To Heather,

God has a plan for everyone's life. And He has unconditional love. Trust Him with all your heart.

This book will show how God can work with someone who trusts Him.

Enjoy

Ron Peters
604-991 1628
RonaldFPeters@gmail.com

Preface

This book is Ron's journey, through sixteen countries. These chapters are intended to give the reader insight, into how wonderful and glorious it is, to be led by the Holy Spirit. (Romans 8:14)

The steps of a good man are ordered by the Lord: and he delighteth in his way. (Psalms 37:23)

The "Webster's New World College Dictionary"
defines missionary
as "sent on a mission" or
"a sending out" or
"being sent out with authority
to perform a special service,
as in preaching, teaching and converting."

The Christian community
around the world,
has people in every church,
wondering what would happen
if they actually uprooted
from where they live,
to become missionaries.

The teachings of King Jesus
point to leaving your comforts, to follow him.
He said:
"my sheep hear my voice,
and I know them,
and they follow me." (St. John 10:27).

Following, is very different from leading.

Exactly what is the missionary experience?

His Royal Majesty King Jesus, Supreme Ruler of
every Galaxy in the Universe, (St. Matthew 28:18)

trained twelve missionaries and sent them out.
But,
before he sent them out,
he gave them power
and authority over all devils,
and to cure diseases.

Then he sent them out to preach
the kingdom of God,

and to heal the sick. (St. Luke 9: 1-5)

His Royal Majesty King Jesus,
also said:

"You have not chosen me,
but I have chosen you,
and ordained you,
that you should

> 1. go (it's not a staying at home suggestion)
>> and
>
> 2. bring forth fruit,
>> and
>
> 3. that your fruit should remain: (monitor and teach them so
>   that they stay saved)

that whatever you shall ask
of the Father in my name,
he may give it you. (St. John 15:16)

Then His Majesty, King Jesus,
trained another seventy missionaries,
and sent them out in pairs. (thirty five pairs).

He gave them the same power.

Then he said unto them
the harvest truly is great,
but the labourers are few:

pray ye therefore
to the Lord of the harvest,
that he would send forth labourers
in his harvest.

Go your ways:
Behold,
I send you forth as lambs among wolves.
(St. Luke 10:1-3)

And into whatsoever city ye enter,
and they receive you,
eat such things as are set before you:
and heal the sick that are therein,
and say unto them:
"the Kingdom of God is come nigh unto you".
 (St. Luke 10: 8-9)

His Royal Majesty King Jesus, also said:

Ye are my friends
if
ye do whatsoever I command you.

Henceforth I call you not servants;

for the servant knoweth not what his Lord doeth:
but I have called you friends;
for all things that I have heard of my Father
I have made known unto you. (St. John 15:14-15)

Being willing to do what he tells you to do,
is critical to hearing his voice.

Hearing his voice
is critical to following him.

Following him and bearing fruit,
is the objective.

Feeding your fruit sufficiently to remain,
is the obligation.

Receiving what you need from the Father,
is the reward.

Once we become friends with the "Supreme Commander" of all the galaxies in the universe, doing what he tells you to do, is easy.

Table of Contents

Preface   v

Chapter 1. My Mother dedicated me before I was born   1

Chapter 2. The California miracles   11

Chapter 3 The Toronto adventure   19

Chapter 4 Money for Egypt   25

Chapter 5 War in Beirut   31

Chapter 6 Damascus, Syria   33

Chapter 7 Amman, Petra and Jericho   35

Chapter 8 Israel   41

Chapter 9 The wonders of Rome   47

Chapter 10 Kelowna to California   49

Chapter 11 Hawaii to Fiji   59

Chapter 12 Tonga (The first time)   65

Chapter 13 New Zealand   79

Chapter 14 Sydney Australia   83

Chapter 15 Singapore   85

Chapter 16 Bangkok   87

Chapter 17 Calcutta   89

Chapter 18 New Delhi   107

Chapter 19 Bombay (now Mumbai)   117

Chapter 20 Kelowna, B.C. Canada   125

Chapter 21 Hawaii   129

Chapter 22 Fiji   133

Chapter 23 Tonga (The second time)   137

Chapter 24 New Zealand   147

Chapter 25 Sydney Australia   155

Chapter 26 Bombay, India   161

Chapter 27 Beautiful Ireland   199

Chapter 28 Kelowna and Edmonton   201

Chapter 29 Vancouver Island   207

Chapter 30 Burnaby and Surrey   211

Chapter 31 North Bay Ontario   215

Chapter 32 Back in Surrey   219

Chapter 33 Promontory, Chilliwack, B.C.   225

Buying the Books   229

CHAPTER 1.
My Mother dedicated me before I was born

Amazing missionary adventures

Most people miss the thinking,
the character, the power,
and the reaction of our great God,
when they read the Holy Bible.
The entire Holy Bible is written for us to understand
how God thinks, and what his relationship is to us.
All of the stories are for us to understand how God
will react in different circumstances.

Everyone saw the reaction of God,
when Pharaoh refused God,
but for some reason,
people today seem to forget,
that the God above us
is the same God.

When a person makes a promise to God, God takes
it seriously, and that promise will be fulfilled.

Hannah wanted a baby,
and she vowed a vow,

and said,
O Lord of Hosts,

if thou wilt indeed look upon the affliction
of thine handmaid,
and remember me,
and not forget thine handmaid,
but wilt give unto thine handmaid a man child,
then will I give him unto the Lord all the days of his life,
and there shall no razor come upon his head.
(I Samuel 1: 11)
The Lord gave Hannah her child and she called him
Samuel (1 Samuel 1:20)
When he was weaned, she took him to Eli the priest,
and said:
For this child I prayed;
and the Lord hath given me my petition
which I asked of him:
therefore also I have lent him to the Lord;
As long as he liveth he shall be lent to the Lord.
And he worshipped the Lord. (1 Samuel 1: 27-28)
Annually, Hannah would visit Samuel who stayed
with the priest.
But Samuel ministered before the Lord, being a
child, girded with a linen ephod.
Moreover his mother made him a little coat, and
brought it to him from year to year, when she came
up with her husband to offer the yearly sacrifice.
(1Samuel 2 : 18-19)

My mother had promised me to God before I was born. She was told that
I would be still born, and they would be lucky to save her life. Then she
prayed, and promised God, that she would dedicate me to the Lord, to
be his servant, and bring me up according to this purpose. She kept her
promise, and from the time I could understand, she began to teach me
about God. When I was five and six years old, she taught me bible verses

and Psalms, and in church, the pastor would hold my hand at the front, on stage, and I would recite these verses Sunday after Sunday. I knew all my life, that I would be a full time servant of God. And I resisted. I looked at the men who were in Gods full time service and thought that I could do way better than that.

I actually thought I'd like to be a medical Doctor.

At eighteen I joined the Airforce to get away from home. I soon found out that military life was not only very boring but was only one step above being on welfare.

All my relatives were financially competitive, and when I was on leave, I determined to get out of the Airforce as quickly as possible. My two best friends left when I did, and we all received an honorable discharge.

Ron at Twenty-three

Albert and I were from Vancouver, B.C., and Barry was from Mortlach, Saskatchewan.

We were twenty-two years old, and full of life. My parents treated us like Kings. It was great to be home. Barry stayed with my parents, and Al went home to his mother. After a few weeks, the pressure started again. My parents were full of love, and constantly told me, that I needed to turn my life over to God.

It was late October, and Barry and I had no money. Foolishly, we decided to hitch hike to Winnipeg to find jobs. We managed to get as far as Kelowna and slept under the steps of an old house. It was really cold and all we had was short, light weight, beige raincoats. The next morning it started snowing and somehow we managed to get rides all the way to Mortlach. We spent the night there and the next morning Barry's Mom and Dad gave us fifty dollars and wished us well.

A crayon salesman gave us a ride to Winnipeg and suggested that Eaton's Catalogue Division were hiring this time of year. We found a cheap room with the fifty dollars, and we both got jobs at Eaton's. The conveyer belts we worked on, had Christmas presents going all over North America, and it was easy to recognize the cookie and chocolate boxes.

We had no money for food, so we lived off of the conveyers for two weeks. After our first paycheques, we managed somewhat better. But it was a while before we managed warmer clothes. Over the next four years we all got better jobs. Al was hired by Canadian Aviation Electronics Industries and was transferred to Winnipeg.

Barry worked for a couple of Finance companies, and I found a job with a personnel consulting company.

For a while, the three of us lived together in the same rooming houses. Then Al got married and was transferred to Toronto. Barry and I moved to Toronto as well. Soon we were all married, and we all bought good houses. On Saturdays, we golfed together.

My cousins in Vancouver were successfully starting their own companies, which provoked me to starting a carpet, tile and linoleum company. It did very well, and soon I started other businesses as well. During this period, my parents would frequently visit with their motor home, and would always leave with the message, that I needed to turn my life over to God. Invariably my response was that I didn't need a crutch in my life. But I was glad that they enjoyed their relationship with God.

When I refused to turn, to the salvation that God was offering me, he turned up the action against me.

First my daughter died of crib death. The

"sudden infant death syndrome" which the professionals call "SIDS". My son was three and my daughter was five months old, when she died. My parents came to the funeral and before they left, they said "God is trying to get your attention."

Unfortunately, my wife heard this, and from that day on, she hated both God and my parents. She wished she had died with our daughter. She wouldn't eat or leave the house. I would come home from work to find her sitting on the floor crying. She was hospitalized for several months and was about 85 pounds. Eventually, she came home, and was still extremely depressed.

Then I had a warehouse accident and was hospitalized for months, with a broken back. During this time, we lost our companies. The bankruptcy courts let us keep everything that was in my wife's name, so when she divorced me, she got the two cars, the house, and our son.

Then my parents were invited to a Full Gospel Businessmen's Banquet, at the Hyatt Regency Hotel in Vancouver. Reluctantly they went, thinking that they could be a testimony to this strange group of "tongue speaking" Christians.

At the end of the session, the speaker invited people to the front, to receive healings. After several people were healed, my wary parents went to the front, and said that they had a son in the hospital in Toronto, who needed healing. The speaker said that my Dad could sit in proxy for me, and they would pray over him, and I would instantly receive my healing in Toronto.

The next day my parents flew to Toronto to witness this miracle. I still couldn't get up because I had no muscles. At first, a nurse exercised me on an inner tube, in pool therapy. It took another 3 weeks of physiotherapy, and then I was released. My parents thought for sure, that now I would become a Christian. But I hardened my heart again, and thought I could easily get a job, and start over.

I was hired immediately, by one of my competitors in the carpet business, and also by an insurance company. My parents left crying, and very bewildered.

Again, I prospered for several months, when one day, my mother called from California and invited me there for a holiday. I told her, "that would be wonderful," to which she responded that: "and on Monday, there is a Full Gospel Businessmen's Convention in the Anaheim Convention Center, and that I was just going to love it." As soon as I heard the word "gospel", I started making excuses why I couldn't come, and my mother immediately said that I shouldn't be so hasty. She said I should sleep on it, and that she would phone me again tomorrow.

The next morning, as I drove into the yard of the Carpet Company, the owner was standing there waiting for me.

He yelled at me to get off his property, and that I was never to come near this place again. Just then, one of my store managers came into the yard and I drove beside him and asked what was wrong. He said, apparently, I had given information on one of our large contracts, that we were tendering, to one of our competitors. I had not done that.

I started to think of how I could defend myself, or perhaps get a lawyer. I drove away, and determined that no matter how this turned out, I would soon start my own carpet company again. I drove to the Insurance Company, and walked to my desk, whereupon my secretary asked why I was so early, and she offered me a coffee. I sat there still perplexed, when the owner walked into my office, and said, that he had just come back from Edmonton. Last night he had sold this insurance company, and the new owners had their own staff, and wouldn't be needing me, but with my experience, and his help, I could easily join another company. He said he wanted to have breakfast with me but had to make a couple of phone calls first.

I was sipping my coffee, when the phone rang, and it was my mother. She said, "Hi Ron, last night there were a couple of hundred Motor Homes gathered early for the convention, and they had an all night prayer meeting, and we were all praying that God would release our loved ones, to be able to come to this convention. I knew it was no use fighting God any longer.

The first night of the convention, Dr. Whitaker from Oklahoma, gave his testimony, and at the end, people were invited to the front, to give their heart to the Lord. I sat between my parents in the first row, and I suppose I was one of the first people up. I had my own personal breakdown, and asked God to forgive me. Hundreds of people were up there with me.

Shortly after, we all said a collective prayer, and we were ushered into another room, where Enoch Christopherson explained the gifts of the Holy Spirit to us. I really didn't understand much of what he said, but at the end, people were putting their hands on my head, and I passed out. When I came to, everyone had gone, except two men, who were now laughing at me. I tried to get up and couldn't. I kept falling down like a drunk. I told them I don't drink. They said, yes, we know. But even when I wasn't saved I didn't drink, and I repeated it again, and finally, they picked me up, with an arm over each one of them, and walked me out to a Denny's restaurant. It was very late, and the place was full. We sat right in the very back, and they ordered three coffees.

Soon I heard a strange sound like birds, and then I noticed an odd man with his hands in the air, whistling like birds, up at the front of the restaurant, near the cash registers. Then this man in a white suit, white shoes, red socks, and a red tie, was walking down the aisle towards us, still whistling like birds. Then suddenly, he stopped at our booth table, and pointed right at me, and said,

"God woke me and told me to go to Denny's and he would show me the man that he wanted me to talk to".

And then the two men that had stayed with me, left, and I was alone with this odd man in the white suit.

His name was George Madrigal. He spent the entire night teaching me about God, about King Jesus, and the gifts of the Holy Spirit. In the morning, he prayed that God would give us energy, as if we had had a full night's sleep, and I felt great all day. I went to the breakfast meeting at seven AM and did not see George again.

Back in Vancouver, I lived with my parents for several months, studying the Bible about 16 hours a day. I just couldn't get enough of it. The Bible was so exciting for me. I was talking to God, and reading the Bible, and I was like a kid at Christmas. One of the best times of my whole life.

Then one day I said to the Lord, "I need to go back into business. I have a strong business acumen, and I'd like to sponsor about a hundred missionaries." The Lord said no, "I want you to go". I responded with, "but then I would have to go to Bible school, and then to Seminary, and then get involved with a church, where I can learn to preach, and eventually they might send me out. It will take so many years". And God said, "I will send you out now".

I was skeptical and said, "but who will let me preach?"

And God said, "I will open the doors for you?"

Then I said, "but what will I preach?" And God said, "I will give you the right words to say".

Then I said, "but what will I do for money?"

And God said, "I will sponsor you".

Then I realized what God was saying, and I bargained one more thing. "But what about my son?" And God said he would always take care of him too.

The first place he sent me, was to Main and Hastings in Vancouver. This is where all the drug addicts, hookers, and criminals hang out. The very first night, God found an indigenous guitar player, who joined me.

The song he sang still brings tears to my eyes.

He sang :

He's never failed me yet,
He's never failed me yet,
Jesus Christ has never failed me yet !
This one thing I know,
Jesus Christ loves me so,
He's never failed,
He's never failed me yet.

Then we both sang loudly, and soon a crowd gathered. Eventually I preached a very simple message. The next night I brought my Guitar as well. Things got better, and we began a ministry that lasted a couple of months. I also got involved with Ron and Vera Ward, who had a daily ministry upstairs, on Hastings Street. It was a church for street people. And the street people received much help. And many received King Jesus' life changing salvation as well.

Shortly after this, I was baptized by Bob Birch at Burnaby Christian Fellowship. Bob had started a church at my parent's home, and it grew and they rented a building. (actually, a fire hall in Burnaby).

Then I became friends with the pastor of a church in Surrey, named Curtis Mitchell. He had a great church, and a radio ministry. He often prophesied and had an anointed preaching. Then I was invited to a minister's Conference at his church, and during this conference I was invited to be ordained. A number of ministers had talked to me, and somehow, they were convinced that I was ready to be ordained. The last day of the convention, I was up on stage, and they laid hands on my head, and prayed, and anointed me, and ordained me. They even gave me the paperwork and certificates.

To this day, not one person anywhere, has ever asked to see my certificates.

CHAPTER 2.
The California miracles

Amazing missionary adventures

Then God told me to go to California. A friend bought me a bus ticket one way to LA, and my brother Stan gave me eighty-four dollars.

My parents had bigger and better things in mind for me. They thought I was being foolish.

Dad gave me a copy of Demos Shakarian's book,

"The happiest people on earth". I finished the book by the time we got to Redding, California, and I gave the book to the young man sitting beside me, that I had led to the Lord, at the beginning of this trip at the bus depot. He left in Redding.

Then a very attractive lady got on the bus, and looked around, and decided to sit right beside me. Thank God I behaved myself and didn't flirt with her. She asked me many questions, and I told her what I did now. She became really interested, and over the next hour, I lead her to the Lord. Turned out, she was an airline stewardess from Russia. She had a couple of days off and decided to tour a bit. She explained how Christianity in Russia was all underground, and very secretive. She had never had any exposure to Christianity, but always knew there was a God. She had so many questions. Our trip to Los Angeles went far too fast. I had two Bibles with me, and I gave her my best one. She could read English, and

I knew this entire trip was orchestrated by the Holy Spirit. She was in a hurry to get to the airport, and we said goodbye.

When we arrived in Los Angeles, the bus Depot was quite weird. They had showers in the basement, but I had a guitar case and a suitcase, and what if someone stole them. Then I realized I was on a mission and had supernatural protection. I had my shower, and went outside, and a demon possessed lady met me outside, and screamed at me. She was barefoot and her feet were bleeding a lot. She was yelling obscenities at me, and then she started saying, what did I come here for. What did I want her. Then she said, "go back to Vancouver".

I said, "the Lord rebuke you Satan", and she ran away. Then the Lord told me to go to "Motel Six".

I had never heard of "Motel Six", so I asked a man where it was. He said the closest one, was north to I-5, and then about 5 miles left, and I would see it there. So he pointed me in the right direction. It took a couple of hours to reach I -5 and I was so tired from carrying my suitcase and guitar case. And I had not slept that well on the Greyhound bus, because I'm tall. So I managed to cross the overpass and come down on the other side to the highway, and I stood there about to hitchhike. I prayed and said, "God, I'm so tired". And immediately God said, "yes I know, I would have given you a ride back there, at the bus station, but you didn't ask me". I started crying because I realized what a friend I had in God.

I stuck my thumb out, and immediately, a brand new copper colored Thunderbird stopped for me. As I ran to this car, the trunk popped open, and I put my things inside, and opened the passenger door. This large red headed man held out his hand and said, "hi, I'm Reverend John Dye". I started crying again. When I stopped, he said, "where are you going" and I said, "to Motel Six".

John said he knew where it was, and within minutes we were there. On the way there, John had asked me all the normal questions. There were people waiting to talk to the man behind the counter. He was telling someone on the phone, "Sorry, we don't have any rooms available. No, we won't have anything for at least 2 months. Sorry, we have so many conventions down here."

Then he said the same thing to the people in line. John said to me, "look, my wife and I just recently married, and we have this big brand new home, and we have extra beds for visiting preachers. We have a fridge full of food, and we'd love to have you stay with us."

I said, "no, there must be a reason why God has sent me here. I have to stay here."

So, John gave me his card, and said I could even call later, and he would come back for me. I have never seen him again.

The man behind the counter was busy with phone calls again, and I sat on this orange vinyl sofa and waited. I prayed and said, "God, what should I do". God just said, "Wait".

You don't know me yet, but I hate waiting.

After about half an hour later, the man behind the counter finished a call and said to me, "There you go, we have just had a cancellation. Just fill out your name and address on this card". I did and he handed me a key. He said, "your lucky, its all paid for, for the next three days" . I was overwhelmed, thanked him, and started crying again, and left.

The room was on the second level, and after I climbed the stairs, I walked down the long outdoor hallway toward my room. There were five Mexican fellows standing there drinking beer. They had tattoos and looked like a gang. My room was just past them, so I carried my guitar and suitcase by them, and went to my room. Inside I cried, and thanked God for this miraculous room. Then I asked "God, why did you send me here"? He said, "go outside".

I did, and immediately was confronted with these five fellows. They were friendly and invited me to have a beer with them. I walked to them, and they asked me the usual questions. Where was I from, and what did I do. I told them I was a priest. Then I asked them, what did they need from God. Instantly they changed. They said they came here for jobs, and there were none.

They were going home tomorrow, and they were just celebrating their last night. I walked in front of them and said follow me. I walked into their room and knelt down, and said, "we are going to pray". I said for them all to hold hands. They did. I joined the hand holding. Then I prayed. Asked God to show us where the jobs were for them. I said to God, that he didn't send me here for nothing, and he didn't send them here for nothing. Then I asked the men, where was the last place you went to?

They told me, and I said, "go there early tomorrow morning, and all five of you are going to get hired".

They asked me if I was sure. I said, yes".

Then I went to my room.

I was wondering why I said that.

What if they didn't get the jobs. I was easy to find.

Then the Holy Spirit reminded me who I was.

Within two minutes, there was noise in the yard, and I went out. The manager of the Motel was yelling for someone to help him. The Mexicans yelled back that I was a priest. They beckoned me to go quickly.

On the floor of the reception area, in the Motel, was a lady, who was obviously choking to death.

She couldn't breathe and the manager was panicking.

Two little children were nearby and crying.

Turned out this lady was the managers wife.

I told him God was going to heal her now.

I knelt beside her and prayed. I put my hands on her forehead, and asked God for his miracle. Nothing happened.

She was sucking in air with a terrible noise, and everyone could tell she was not doing well.

People kept coming into this small room, and every time, they would ask, "what's wrong with the lady." At first it was me that replied. I said, "God is healing her." Then the manager started to repeat it, to these strangers, who had come here for a room.

"It's OK, God is healing her." Sure didn't look like God was healing her. It took so long. And everyone was thinking, this isn't working. Should we call an ambulance. The Mexican fellows said to someone, he's a priest. I kept thinking that "what if she doesn't make it." It seemed like half an hour had passed. It was probably half that, but I was praying in tongues and under my breath, asking God to hurry.

Then suddenly she got up and was breathing normally.

Now I took control.

I told everyone to kneel down, and we were going to thank God, for healing this lady. I said to the man in the back, "Sir, please put out your cigar. Just kneel down."

And now I prayed my salvation prayer. Of course we thanked God for his miracle. Then I thanked him for our salvation. I went through the entire sinner's prayer and by the end many were crying. When they left, the wife asked, if I would have breakfast with them.

Sometime after six o'clock in the afternoon, the Mexicans came back. They found me and proclaimed that God did it. They had jobs and were not going home. I asked the manager, if it would be alright to have a bible study, by the pool. He said, "that would be fine", and the first night, about twenty people joined us. I played guitar and sang, and they joined in. Then I got people to tell their story. It was amazing how many needed urgent prayer. After each story, I prayed over that individual for a miracle. It was very emotional. The next night people brought friends. For me, it was a new way of preaching. God had promised to open the doors, and to give me the right words, but I never thought it would be like this. This was the beginning of a template, that God had me use all over the world.

Someone knew an older lady and invited her to our meetings. She looked wealthy, and it turned out that she was the president of a bank. She had also started a small church in that bank. And I was invited to come and do the Sunday morning service. She said she would have someone come and pick me up.

It really was different. She arrived, just as this man and I arrived, and she opened up the bank, and reset the alarms and people started to come in. Chairs were spread around from some back room. I stood in the front with my guitar and bible. I placed my Bible on the counter and started playing my old song again. "He's never failed me yet." I started crying, and other people started crying, and the Holy Spirit came down. God showed me that some needed healing, and I started praying over individuals. The bank lady was one of them. She had arthritis and was in considerable pain. The pain left, and she showed everyone. That opened many more doors. She knew a lot of church pastors, and I got invited. I thought God was sending me on a theological mission because I had studied so hard. I thought I might be impressive.

God thought that my work should be practical.

I did very little teaching. I did read the Word of God, but the practical side was always the thrust.

People wanted to see God action. I was busy every day.

All the way down to La Jolla, and El Cajon and eventually Mexico.

I was invited to people's homes, and that was of God as well.

In San Diego, a pilot came to one of the meetings. He had flown Jumbo 747 Jets, and when he retired he became blind. Now they all expected God to heal him. Me too. But I prayed fervently, and nothing happened. I wondered, "God, why didn't you do it. It would have been so good for my integrity."

Two days later, at a Full Gospel Businessmen's luncheon in Santa Anna, my pilot showed up. With an entourage. He was invited to come up and speak a few words, and he kind of took over. A man of authority. Both eyes were perfect. Some years later he and his wife came to a 10 day conference I held in Hawaii, and they got to meet Isobel and my parents.

At this meeting in Santa Ana, I met a Doctor of Physics (PHD) who invited me to stay with his wife and him, in Tustin. He and two other Doctors (one had a PHD in Mathematics and the other had a PHD in Chemistry.) worked together in a Lab in LA. They were inventing a better way to produce Ozone, as a propellant. It was their habit to stop at "Melodyland" every morning, for the prayer meeting at 5:00 am. About 200 to 300 men showed up every morning.

The pastor was Ralph Wilkerson.

Many times the Lord had already had me Prophecy to people, and one morning, I had a prophecy for Ralph Wilkerson. He was the brother to David Wilkerson of New York, who wrote the "Cross and the Switchblade". At this time, Ralph had a huge church on Harbour Boulevard across from Disney land. Melodyland was formerly "a theatre in the round". Ralph had made this church really special. All the great preachers came there. But what I liked best about this church, was that, at every service, they would have an alter call, and then they would take the converts to the top, in the back, and baptize them. My theology. "Those that believe and are baptized shall be saved." (St. Mark 16:16)

Melodyland had a drug rehabilitation program, a preschool, a daycare, a high school, and the "Melodyland School of Theology". Today, the Lord gave me a word of prophecy for Ralph. I said to him, "Thus saith the Lord, you will leave Melodyland and begin a new work with street people."

I actually hated that I had to say that to him. He was so successful, in what he had accomplished at Melodyland. Amazingly, he already knew that he was leaving.

Mexico was very different. Mostly they were poor.

I was amazed at how they actually lived. In Canada, I could have bought everything they owned, for less than a thousand dollars. And yet they were generous. They gave me a bed. They fed me. Their food had peppers in it. My eyes would water. I stayed in several homes.

I worked my way down the Baja Peninsula.

The desert was really hot, and the people had almost nothing. This is where I needed to learn, what they actually needed from God.

Working with an interpreter every where I went, was also a learning curve for me.

Much of my teaching concerned water baptism. It was actually a challenge to baptize them. But they were willing to please God. In some places I also taught about the Holy Spirit. Some accepted. They accepted because I told them they needed power to heal people, and to speak in tongues for power praying.

I also learned about flash flooding in the desert sand.

Rivers form within minutes, and you need to get to high ground very quickly.

I don't think I ran into any families that didn't need prayer. Because of where they live, there are many limitations. I really enjoyed the people of Mexico. Perhaps God will send me back to Mexico again.

CHAPTER 3
The Toronto adventure

Amazing missionary adventures

On the way back, God instructed me to go to Toronto.

I travelled by bus.

As we were leaving Albuquerque, New Mexico, there was a very long hill, and it was snowing. I sat behind the bus driver and our bus was full. We were driving uphill, and cars were sliding everywhere. I began to pray out loud. I even raised my hands, and said, "God help our bus get up the hill safely. All of a sudden, I saw a car sliding out of control, right towards our bus. I quickly said, "God straighten that car out so that it won't hit us." It was just like a giant hand took the car and put it back in the down hill lane. But then, more cars were sliding. I prayed loudly again and said, God help everyone to be safe in this snow. It was snowing big snowflakes and really hard. Then I realized I was praying wrong. Again I prayed and said, "God, in Jesus name, stop the snow". In 10 seconds it was suddenly sunny and no snow. It was like we had driven into another world. The Bus driver grabbed his microphone and said, " Did you all hear that. This guy behind me prayed and the snow stopped instantly. Wow, did you all see that ?"

I had tears in my eyes and in my voice.

I took my cue. I stood up into the aisle, and said,

"We all need to pray now, and thank God for his miracle. Just pray after me. Father, in Jesus name, thank-you for saving our lives. Thank you for stopping the snow, so we could be safe. Thank you for stopping the snow, so that everyone would be safe. Thank you God that you are real and that you care about us. Thank you God for your gift of salvation. Amen".

Then I spent almost an hour teaching. At the end we had a salvation meeting. They prayed with me again.

Toronto was also miraculous. I was wondering why God sent me out of the way to Toronto. I walked out of the Bus depot, and saw the Four Seasons Hotel two blocks away, and thought they would have a nice clean washroom. As I walked through the doors, there was a huge banner hanging from the ceiling, which read, "His banner over us is love." They were here.

The "Full Gospel Businessmen" were having the Canadian convention here. I found a washroom and changed. When I came out, a concierge offered to take my guitar and suitcase, and store them. He gave me a ticket for my luggage. I was hungry, and he directed me to a restaurant upstairs. He said they were all up there. Indeed they were. A long lineup.

I got in line. I only had about five dollars, but I thought I might get something. A huge man was in front of me, and within seconds, he turned around and said, Hi, I'm Karl from Peterborough. Where are you from.

I began to tell him, and he took great interest in my latest adventures. He asked if I was staying in this hotel, and I said that I hadn't booked anything yet. He said, "oh that's great. I had booked ahead by phone, and when they asked me what kind of room I wanted, I said, just give me one of your best rooms. When I went up to my room, it turned out to have three beds, and sofas, and two bathrooms, and a small kitchen. I'm all by myself, so how would you like to stay with me." I said, "sorry, but I don't have any money". "Oh I don't want your money; I just hate to see the beds go to waste.

That settles it . You're with me. You really don't have any money". I said no. "Tell me more of what you have been doing". So I told him some of the stories.

He was fascinated. When we got near the front, about to be seated, he said, "Ron, take one of my credit cards, and at every meal, invite people to join you, and you pay for them all. Tell them what you've been telling me". He gave me an American Express card.

I soon met other people, and then, one of the men I met, who sat with us, said "you need to be one of our speakers." During the next three days, I not only was given the chance to speak in front of the whole crowd, but I also got to minister to many people individually.

At the end of the convention, Karl found me, and I gave him the credit card, and all the receipts, and he thanked me for using his card. 'Said he would get a blessing from it.

Then a very distinguished man came to me, and said, "I hear you need to get to Vancouver. I'm a car dealer, and I have two new Lincolns that I need to drive back to Vancouver. Would you drive one for me?" I said, I would have to pray about that, to which he said, "I need to know within the next half hour."

Five minutes later another man I had befriended came to me. He was an evangelist from somewhere in Mexico, but he had an engagement in Vancouver next week, and was driving a Volkswagen Beetle to Vancouver, and just wanted the company.

I said to him, "give me half an hour to pray about it".

He agreed and left. I went down the escalators and sat on a sofa on the main floor. I started praying.

I asked God to make the choice for me. Within minutes, God said neither. I was confused because I really thought that God had arranged these two choices for me. Now I had to go and tell both men, that I wasn't going with them. The car dealer thought I was being very foolish and even offered me three hundred dollars to drive for him. He left after I apologized.

Then the evangelist with the VW came to me, and he was very disappointed. He didn't think I was hearing from God. I was beginning to wonder as well, if I was really hearing from God.

Then I prayed again, and God told me to go back downstairs and sit on that same sofa. People were leaving the Hotel, and soon it seemed like everyone had gone home. I sat there wondering why I was still there. God just said "wait".

I did. The Concierge gave me my luggage, and I sat there. Almost an hour had gone by, when suddenly some people came out of the elevator in front of me and started to walk toward the door. It was like they couldn't see me.

And just like that, the man turned around and said to me, "you don't need a room for the night, do you"? I said, "yes", and he threw me the key, and told me the room number, and said he was a pastor in Oshawa, and had planned to stay the night, but someone in his church was dying, and he had to rush back home. And just as quickly he was gone.

I started to cry, and thanked God, and got up to go to the room. God told me to stay on the sofa, and just wait. Now I was confused. And within two minutes a bellman came to me and asked why I was sitting there. I said I was waiting for someone. When he left, I wondered if I had lied. I wasn't sure about anything now. I waited and prayed and wondered what was going to happen next.

It took over an hour, and suddenly, I heard the front door open, and when I looked, there was an old man standing there, looking around the room. When he saw me, he started to run towards me. A very awkward old man, running toward me. He was all out of breath, and said, "you must be the man". He said, "do you have any money", to which I said, "no". He was relieved and said, "you must be the right man". And he reached into his jacket pockets and pulled out several rolls of money. He said "here, the Lord told me to rush to Toronto, and find you here, and give you all my money".

I said, "who are you." And he said, "I'm Frank Smith from Kitchener". I said, "Frank are you a rich man?" To which he said, "no, but I keep some money in jars in my kitchen, and the Lord told me to take it all, and bring it to you". By this time I was crying again. Frank said, "I've got to go now", and I shook his hand, and thanked him for his blessing.

And he walked out of the door and was gone.

I was in shock. I tried several times over the years to find Frank, and never did locate him.

The next morning God told me to get a bus to Vancouver.

I slept on the bus, and it was cold and snowing through Manitoba. The Greyhound bus didn't have a good heater, and it was below zero outside. Somewhere in Saskatchewan, our bus suddenly stopped. The driver went outside to determine the problem, and when he came back, he announced that the motor was frozen. He was going to walk to a restaurant that we had passed, to get help. He insisted that we all stay in the bus, so we wouldn't freeze. This was before cell phones, and there wouldn't have been any service out there anyway.

The driver left, and within minutes the bus started to get very cold.

I prayed and God told me to take the people down the road, to the restaurant. I presented myself and told them we would perish if we stayed. I suggested that everyone get out their suitcases and put on everything warm that they could find. Some of the men started bringing in the suitcases from below, and everyone dressed. I made everyone hurry. Then I led them down the road. I had two men at the back checking on stragglers. It was windy and snowing and terrible. We walked about two miles like that, and toward the end, several of us were helping others, with arms around our necks. Then I saw a light, and within minutes we were there. The lady had actually closed that afternoon but had opened for the bus driver and now she made a huge pot of hot chocolate. We had made it. I got everyone in a circle, and said I was going to pray to God, for saving us. We could have frozen to death. It took several hours, and we finally got another bus. People confessed, that they actually thought we were all going to die.

I talked to them about some of my experiences and told them how real God was.

God had opened another door.

CHAPTER 4
Money for Egypt

Amazing missionary adventures

I asked God if I could go back to work.

God said I should drive taxi. To me that was the lowest job possible. But I obeyed God. I moved to a small apartment on 11th Ave., near Granville in Vancouver, and got a job at MacLure's Cabs. I drove taxi a few days a week and studied Bible in all of my free time. After a few weeks, I began working with several bible study groups. I had one at the Pentecostal church in Richmond. One near marine drive, in Vancouver with Mennonites. One in Langley near the highway and 200 Street. One in Abbotsford every Tuesday morning, with Dutch Reform ladies only. In between I drove taxi for my living.

One day, I met a pastor and his wife, who had a church upstairs, in the next building to MacLure's Cabs. Frank Pace and his wife Vanessa had come from Hillsboro, Kansas, to start a ministry in Vancouver. Frank asked me to preach on a Sunday morning, and I did. But I never got a chance to go back. For some reason the church closed down, and I lost track of Frank.

I had many experiences driving taxi, that God privileged me with. Here are three.

I was driving on the Lions gate bridge late at night, when near the center of the bridge, I saw something on the railing. When I got closer, I saw a man in a sleeping bag, sitting on the railing, with his legs in the bag, on the outside of the railing. He was committing suicide. I jumped out of the car and ran to him, and just as he decided to push himself over, I grabbed the bag near the top, and started pulling him back. He was very heavy, but I was stronger in those days. He almost pulled me over with him. It was close. But God helped me, and I managed to save him. Turned out, that he had been at a drinking party under the bridge, and his friends had dared him to jump. For some reason, he was too embarrassed to refuse his friends. I called the police, and they took him away. The police had me make a report.

A few days later his parents phoned me, to thank me.

Another time I was at the corner of Main and Hastings when I saw a man come out of a Hotel bar, and collapse on the sidewalk. I drove quickly in front of him and jumped out to help. He had several stab wounds in his stomach and was bleeding out of those holes. I had to make a quick choice. If I called an Ambulance, they would get there in time to see him die. Or I could take him to St. Paul's Hospital, and get blood all over my car, and give him a chance to live. I quickly put him in my car and drove too fast to the hospital. In emergency, they rushed him to an operating room, and I stayed to hear the result. The police were also coming to interview me. This guy made it, and I actually saw him a few months later on the street. He didn't know who I was. I tried to talk to him and got nowhere. I wanted to talk to him about Jesus. I don't always win.

Another time a prostitute flagged me, on Main Street, and we started talking. She was very young. Eventually she told me her pimp was her cousin. He invited her down from Queen Charlotte Islands, and she thought it was going to be toward a real job. But he got her hooked on drugs, and then put her to work. She was crying, and I said, "why don't you go home to your parents." She said, "he never lets me keep any money". I asked if she would go right now if I gave her the money. She agreed, and I drove her to the bus depot, and also gave her enough money to take the ferry from Prince Rupert. I watched her get on to the bus still crying.

'Never saw her again.

After several months, God told me to go to Egypt.

I had no extra money. God said to go and book a ticket. Somehow, Eaton's came into my head, and

I walked to Eaton's, and they had a small travel agency in the basement. Molly showed me a tour for Egypt, that also went to Lebanon, Syria, Jordan, Israel, and Rome. I prayed, and God told me to book it. The trip was exactly $ 2500.00.

Molly let me fill out the forms, and then asked me how I was intending to pay for it. The tour was leaving on Friday, a week from now. I told her I'd have the money, but I had not brought it with me. She said, "why should I trust you". And I said, I was a minister. She said, "You must have the money by Wednesday". Wednesday afternoon, we give the tickets back to the airlines to sell.

I went home, and asked God, who I should phone, to get the money. God said, "no one".

Over the weekend I became very anxious. I asked God what should I do, and he said, "just wait".

I'm still not very good at waiting. By Sunday, I began to fast, and prayed fervently, on my knees. I was packed and ready to go on Friday, but waiting was hard. Didn't even know what I was waiting for.

Monday I got a phone call from George Madrigal, who had met me the night I got saved. He was the man at Denny's in Anaheim, CA. George said he needed a new pair of shoes, and God had told him, that I would help him. I was tempted to give him all of my excuses, but I didn't. George gave me all his details, and I went to Western Union, and sent him the money.

I still needed the money for Wednesday, for Molly.

Tuesday night, I got angry. "How could I misunderstand you so badly, God. How can we work together, when I can't even communicate properly."

Then I cried a lot. Later God said, "why are you worrying. Have I ever let you down?"

Now I was really ashamed. I apologized. Asked God to forgive me. But I was still wondering, how I was going to pay Molly tomorrow. Wednesday came and no money. Molly phoned me and was really upset with me. "You call yourself a minister. You should be ashamed of yourself." And I was. I was numb.

Nothing happened all day.

Thursday morning there was a knock on my door, and a lady from the Abbotsford Bible Study was standing there. She came in, and told me her story.

On Tuesday, when I didn't come to the Bible study,

(I had phoned Monday and said that I couldn't make it) she said that, at the end of the meeting, they prayed like they always do, and one of the ladies spoke up, and said, "I think God wants us to bring all the money in our bank account to Ron". Immediately another lady spoke up and said the same thing.

They all agreed, and this lady was the treasurer, and went to the bank for a cheque. They always had a collection at the end of every meeting. When they had opened the bank account, they had trouble deciding on the name on the account, so they finally agreed to call it "Jesus Christ, King of Kings"

So now this lady in front of me, handed me a cheque and asked me what I would do with it. She didn't know what I needed it for. I looked at the cheque, and it was a certified bank cheque, printed "Jesus Christ, King of Kings" for exactly $ 2,500.00. I explained to her why I was crying, and what I needed it for. We were both overwhelmed. She left, and I ran down to Eaton's to see Molly. Molly looked at me in disgust, and said, "I told you, on Wednesday, we gave all the tickets back to the Airline." I begged her to try, and still book me on that tour.

She turned around, and went to the back, and got on the phone. Fifteen minutes later, she came back with a ticket for me, and I gave her the cheque. You are an amazing guy. You must have some connections. We are never allowed to do this.

She was right. I do have some connections.

That Friday, I was on a plane to London, England.

What I haven't told you, is that while I was in California, I realized that people had no way of knowing who I was, and what I was there for. So, back in Vancouver (actually in Burnaby on Kingsway) I found a Bible Store that sold priest shirts. I bought several. 3 beige, and 3 navy blue with those little white plastic fronts, that fit into the collar.

Now everyone knew who I was. And it brought me a lot of God business. People would come up to me, and ask, "can you pray for my daughter, she ran away from home on Monday"

So here I was on the plane, and who did God plant beside me for nine hours, but a Catholic priest named John. I had my collar on, and so did he. He wanted to know all of my stories, and I wanted to know all of his. We were instant friends.

We had expected to leave London about an hour after we arrived. We had about an eight hour delay. October 6,1981, President Anwar Sadat was assassinated in Cairo. When we landed in Cairo, the entire Airport was in siege. Everyone was under suspicion. Even though the assassins were either caught or killed, the people of authority were still in shock and afraid. The soldiers were disorganized because no one had expected this. The man checking my passport, obviously had no English, and spent half an hour, with my passport upside down.

At no time did I try to correct him. We finally were taken to a hotel and were glad to be safe. For the next week, John and I walked the streets, and prayed with many wonderful people. We were never afraid. We also got a trip into the country, where people were very poor. Hundreds of apartment blocks had been erected by Sadat's government, but they couldn't get materials fast enough. People had moved in anyway. They lived in apartments with no walls. Most of the hundreds of three story apartment blocks, had no outside walls.

Families lived like that, with children, and could easily fall two or three stories down, because the outside walls were missing. Sometimes bricks and concrete were rationed, and people would build six feet of wall, two feet high, and hardly any concrete. They needed places to live and were patient.

We also went to the Pyramids. One of the worst things I have done in my life, was to enter the Cheops, also known as the "Cheops pyramid" of Khufu the Pharaoh, at Giza, Cairo, Egypt. The entrance is at 17 meters high, and I had to climb those huge stones, to get to the entrance. John refused to come with me. A heights thing. The base of the pyramid is 227 meters, and the height was originally 147 meters. There is a shaft that goes up to the kings burial chamber, and at that time it was primitive, with two small light bulbs for this very long shaft (took almost an hour to go up this shaft. and it was very narrow and stunk horribly because of the lack of air and oxygen. It would be worse for people that suffer from claustrophobia or have heart problems. Most of the way, the shaft is very low, so that you need to climb bent over, to climb the steps. But the pyramids are very impressive. And there are tunnels everywhere.

Then we flew to Beirut.

CHAPTER 5
War in Beirut

Amazing missionary adventures

It took us a while to land in Beirut because the runway had house size bombing holes on and near the runway. We landed with our heads bowed to our knees and prayed. We were rushed from the plane to a room, in the second basement. We stayed there for more than an hour, during which time John and I prayed with the people, all holding hands. It was of God. We got every one to repeat the words after me. Some were so overwhelmed, they were crying.

Then John and I and the flight crew, were asked to follow someone, and outside, we were rushed into a van. The driver was terrified and drove around all obstacles. On the sidewalk, around other vehicles and far too fast. We were being shot at. When we arrived at our Hotel, we noticed five new bullet holes on the side of the van, and yet no one had been hit.

The elevator was in the center of the bombed out building, and we got off at the eleventh floor. That is where the reception desk now was. We checked in, and John and I were sent into the same room. John had already begun to question my doctrine, on water baptism. Now he wanted to know more. I knew where he was headed. I had talked about the miracles of healing, and he needed to know more. We were up all night, and at the end he was baptized by the Holy Spirit and spoke in tongues.

This changed everything.

We spent a few days walking around Beirut. Every day, there was machine gun fire in the streets. But I told John, God didn't send us here to die. He could have done that back home. We prayed with many people in their homes. They were afraid, and we comforted them. Told them how real God was.

Our Hotel looked down at the beach, which was now full of garbage. And barbed wire. Our hotel was at five corners, and watching the traffic from fourteen floors up, was amazing. Can you imagine cars from five streets coming together at an intersection, and everyone panicking to get out of there, because of the gun fire.

John and I knew that we were there to minister.

Beirut is much like Jerusalem. There are Moslems and Jews and Christians. The press and media want us to think that they all hate each other, but that is not true. They have lived together for hundreds of years. Their children play together. Both in Beirut and in Jerusalem. The shop keepers know everyone. And everyone was very friendly to John and I. Even when bullets were flying around, people invited us into their homes, and would offer us food and drink. We would talk, and then we would pray for them. It didn't matter that most of them weren't Christian. I wish we could tell you, that I led some to become Christians. But that didn't happen. We did pray for sick. Beirut has well over two million people, and we walked everywhere. Most street corners had sandbags about five feet high in a circle. And soldiers with machine guns were staying down low, and occasionally took some shots. We didn't see anyone get hit. We did see bombs land and blow up the side of a building. John and I were not afraid. I told him if we die here, God loses two of his soldiers. He's not that kind of a God. We still have much work ahead of us. We could have died when the plane landed.

CHAPTER 6
Damascus, Syria

Amazing missionary adventures

We took a bus to Damascus. Not a very nice bus.

Damascus is one of the oldest cities in the world.

The main Roman road today is called "Souq Midhat Pasha", and is the street mentioned in Acts 9:11 called "Straight Street' where Ananias went to the house of Judas, to meet blind "Saul of Tarsus". The street signs still say, "Straight Street."

We were in that house and also Ananias house.

Two thousand year old houses.

Syria has five Cathedrals.

"St. Mary's of the Holy Belt Cathedral" in Homs.

"St. Elias Maronite Cathedral" in Aleppo.

"Forty Martyrs Cathedral" in Aleppo.

"Cathedral of our Lady of the Dormition" in Damascus.

"Syriac Catholic Cathedral of St. Paul" in Damascus.

Christianity is embedded here, but not open to change.

They don't want to learn anything more.

The dominant religion of Syria is still Muslim.

Both religions are very political.

John and I never really got to Minister here.

But the fact that it was all real Christian history,

and that it was two thousand years old,

made it very interesting.

I had trouble with the food.

CHAPTER 7
Amman, Petra and Jericho

Amazing missionary adventures

In Amman, Jordan, we stayed at a nice Hotel about five miles from the airport. The food was much better, and the people were friendly.

The next day we went by bus to Petra. Not many miles before Petra, we came to that Rock, where Moses had hit the rock twice, and water came out for everyone. That water is still flowing out of the rock, and it is "cold and delicious".

Nothing grows in that area. The place is called "Meribah".

(Numbers 20:7-12) But Moses was told just to speak to the rock. He disobeyed the Lord. Their punishment was, (both Moses and Aaron) that they would not be going into the promised land called Israel.

God said: "because you believed me not".

I resolved right there, to be very careful in obeying God precisely, and exactly, from now on. We have the same God Moses had, and God doesn't change. (Malachi 3: 6)

I get strange thoughts sometimes. You know the way in a parade, there might be someone carrying a large sign, which has some provocative slogan on it. Well, I was thinking that I should have someone with that kind of sign, going ahead of me, saying:

"Don't mess with God".

A bit further, we came to the Sodom and Gomora area. Round charcoal rocks 3 feet high, and in very straight columns, about eight feet apart, in uniform formation, about 300 feet wide, and many miles long.

Why google has no pictures of the rocks we saw, is a mystery to me. Perhaps they were useful for their composition, and some company gathered them all up, and trucked them away.

It has been forty-two years since I saw them.

Petra is a four hour bus ride from Amman. Petra in the Bible was called "Selah". When Amaziah, the King of Judah defeated Sela by war, he renamed it, and called it "Joktheel". (2 Kings 14: 7-8)

We rode horses down the narrow gorge entrance. (about 10 feet wide and a kilometer long.) The city at the bottom is wide and was totally independent of the outside world. When I was there, people lived there, with sheep and chickens. And they had water. Every building is hand carved into the red rock, in the most artistic way.

Petra is very beautiful.

I preached on the stage of the amphitheatre, at the far end of Petra. I remember staring in awe at every building, thinking of how they had to chisel the stone for every part, of every building, by hand. Years later, I watched a "You Tube movie" on how they could have done that.

On the last day, at our Hotel in Amman, Jordan, we were scheduled to bus to the airport, and then bus to Jericho. But God had a plan for me. I was actually broke. I had used all of my money. But I knew God would take care of me because he had promised. We were waiting for our bus to arrive, to go to the airport, when someone got on a microphone and made an announcement. There had been a plane crash at the airport, and the airport was closed down until further notice. All of us had already checked out of our rooms.

I sat at a small table, on the side of the large lobby, and read my Bible. It happened quite suddenly. A very nice man came beside me and said, "is that a Bible you are reading?" I confirmed that, and he asked to join me. He said, "I have something to ask you. My wife and I are from the U.S.A., and we came in hope of fixing our marriage. We have not been getting along, and we were hoping this second honeymoon would help. It hasn't. I don't want to divorce. We talked for an hour, and I led him through a prayer. Then his wife found us, and we all held hands and prayed again. He gave me his phone number, and shortly after that, our bus driver announced that it was alright to go to the airport now. That couple were going to Petra.

On the bus, which was going by the airport, and then on to Jerico, I reached into my jacket pocket, and found a roll of American money.

We were told that the plane that had delayed us, had about two feet of wing ripped off. The rest of the plane was fine. God had done a miracle, so that a marriage could be saved.

The Jerico wall was amazing. I had reread the Bible story and explained it to the people with us. (Joshua 6:1-27).

Then we crossed the border into Israel. A terrible experience because we were coming from Arab states into Israel. Machine guns everywhere, and they made us strip, and kept us for hours. They searched everything.

Then on the other side, we were taken up the hill to a restaurant, in the "Russian Museum and Park" complex in Jericho. Many buses were parked across the street from the stone-concrete wall surrounding the park. Zacchaeus' tree was on a hill, just before the restaurant and park. A huge Sycamore-fig tree that Zacchaeus had climbed to see Jesus passing. (St. Luke 19 :1-10)

I stood and prayed there, while the others lined up for chicken. Hundreds of people were there. I asked God, why so little ministry had been accomplished by us in Syria and Jordan. All God said was, "be patient".

After eating, I went and sat on the outside curved concrete wall and prayed. Many people were returning and going back to the buses. I was watching an older couple walking very slowly, behind the buses, looking for their bus. Suddenly our bus started rolling towards me, right where this couple was walking. She made it. He didn't. I can still hear the crunching of his bones, as the bus rolled over him. There was screaming and panic.

Our bus driver came running and got into his bus and started it up. Then very slowly, with other men telling him what to do, he drove forward.

More crunching and lots of blood. Then many men yelled, and a very old pickup truck, like a model A Ford, came there. They loaded this man onto it. I stopped them and said we must pray, or he'll die. I laid my hands on him and prayed a healing prayer and also in tongues. Then they drove away.

The police were everywhere. No one was allowed to leave, and they arrested our driver. Everyone was crying. Many surrounded me. I told everyone, "why do you think this happened here?" This is where Jesus was teaching. This is Holy Ground. Jesus still does miracles. That man is going to be alright.

Then I started to think, why did I say that.

What if he dies. He was extremely crushed and bleeding and unconscious. They kept us for several hours.

The police were questioning everyone.

Since I saw it all, I gave a witness statement. I reminded the police that the bus had not moved, but had remained totally still, for more than an hour, before the accident. It may have been sabotaged. Jericho was originally part of Syria.

No one was able to leave.

Then a vehicle drove up to the park, and the man who was crushed, walked towards us, and raised his shirt. He was fine. I got everyone to hold hands in a huge circle, and we thanked God for his miracle.

Many were crying again.

CHAPTER 8
Israel

Amazing missionary adventures

Our hotel was in Jerusalem. I could talk for days about Jerusalem. I'd love to be a tourist guide there.

I've been to every part of Israel.

We went to the tomb of Lazarus. That was very emotional for me.

On the east side of the walls of Jerusalem, is the Kidron Valley. If you go out of the Dung Gate and left, down to the end of the long hill, you come to Absalom's Tomb in front of the Jehoshaphat cave, near the tomb of Zechariah. On the other side of the tomb, if you go up the very long hill, you come to the garden of Gethsemane, with the eight olive trees, where Jesus prayed, before he was arrested. Further past the garden, is where Jesus ascended back to heaven.

The night Jesus was arrested, they took him straight across the Kidron valley, and up to Caiaphas' (the High Priest) house. There are more than a hundred steps going up. They built a most beautiful church over Caiaphas house, called "the Church of Gallicantu" It has four levels; the upper church, the middle church, the guard room, and the dungeon.

When I was there, a lady from England, Ruth Heflin, was the pastor of a large congregation, and every Sunday, she would move all the Catholic benches to the center of the room, and the people would dance all around the church with their hands raised, worshipping God, and singing very beautifully.

Many also weeping with joy.

Inside of the church at the front, was a very large stone, the size of a house, and to the right side, there was a walkway and eventually steps cut into the rock, going down. There was a large room, and then more steps going down to the guardroom, and then more steps down to the dungeon.

All of this was hewn out of the rock.

And now, I was in the dungeon, and was told, this is where they beat Jesus, and put the thorns on him.

To the right side, were the cells . I remember three of them. The first one, near the steps, is where they kept Jesus. The bull pen was to the left side from the steps, and there were metal rings on the walls where prisoners had been chained.

I wasn't sure that all, of what I had been told, was true.

Then I went into Jesus' cell, and sat down, and the Holy Spirit came on me, and I couldn't stop crying. I was there for a long time, and also had a vision.

I could see it all happening.

I saw how badly he was beaten.

Out of the west side of Jerusalem, is a road to Emmaus. This is where Jesus met the two men, as they were walking and talking, about the recent events about Jesus' crucifixion, and they were bewildered that Mary Magdalene, and Joanna, and Mary, the mother of James, had been at the empty tomb, and said the stone had been rolled away. And after they took Jesus into their home, and fed him, Jesus finally showed them who he was, and then he disappeared.

An hour and half down this road, is Mt. Carmel, where Elijah had his alter contest, against the priests of Baal. Near the alter site, there is a stone cave there, and a church has its services in there. I preached all about Elijah, in that cave church.

Down the mountain, is Tel Aviv. Heading north is a beautiful resort town called Natanya, where our tour group stayed three days. It was very much like San Clemente in California. Sidewalk café's, tourist shops , all downhill toward the beach at the Mediterranean Sea.

On the left side of Tel Aviv, is a suburb called Joppa, where Peter raised up Tabitha from the dead. (the Acts 9:36-41)

The roof top (of a house in Joppa) where Simon Peter had his vision of the great sheet knit at the four corners, is still there for tourists. (The Acts 10: 9-16)

About thirty five kilometers north of Haifa, is Caesarea, (an hour's bus ride), where there is a large chariot circus, like Ben Hur, and a huge amphitheatre. Haifa and Tel Aviv and Caesarea are all along the Mediterranean Sea.

This Amphitheatre is right on the ocean. In the last row, at the top seats, you can hear a match being struck on the stage below. The Mediterranean Ocean is behind it. I preached there also, on that fabulous stage. The tourists were already sitting there, so why not preach. I taught about the reason that King Jesus came to Israel as a baby, and what his mission was, and what he did while he was here.

There are two walled cities in Israel that really impressed me. Of course one is Jerusalem, that Solomon built.

And the other is Acre (formerly Old Akko) to the far west, on the Mediterranean.

Both have interesting wall cut-outs at the top. When you are standing on the inside of the wall at the top, these wall cut-outs have protection from the enemy that would have been shooting from the outside.

Jerusalem has small openings about fifteen inches wide on the outside and six feet wide on the inside .

They are for bowmen to shoot there bow and arrows at the enemy below. These walls are over thirty nine feet high and over eight feet thick.

Old Akko has the opposite. The narrow opening of about twenty four inches is on the inside and about eight feet on the outside. This was for Napoleons cannons to shoot at enemy Navy's below the wall.

I still had my Guitar with me, and at Tiberius there was a wonderful, very wide bricked walkway at the Sea of Galilee, and a three foot ledge to sit on.

I began to play my guitar there, and within minutes, I had over a hundred young military people join me, (both young men and young women), with machine guns over their shoulders. I sang songs that they could join in, and sing with me, and they loved it . Eventually I told where I was from, and then my version about the Messiah. They listened. I told them why Jesus had to come to Israel. I told them how real Jesus is, and that he can forgive them all of their sins. In the end, I had everyone kneel and pray with me. I also prayed a blessing on them, for God to protect them in everything they would be doing.

The next day we were around the left side of the lake, (the Sea of Galilea), where Peter had his house. There are also the remnants of a large Synagogue there. And below, at the sea, there were huge rocks the size of cars, all over the hillside. And on the other side of the road is the beach, where Peter had always launched his fishing boat. All around the hillside, were the most wonderful orange trees. I told everyone to grab an orange and go sit on one of the rocks. If you don't already know, those big Jaffe oranges are phenomenal. Then I went down to the road, across from the lake, and started telling stories of what happened here two thousand years ago. How Jesus saw the disciples out fishing, and yelled at them, to cast the net to the other side. And Peter counted one hundred and fifty three fish, when they came to shore.

Also, how Jesus walked on the water in a storm toward the disciples in their boat, and then stretched forth his hand and caught Peter who became afraid and began to sink, when he tried to walk on the water too.

And how Jesus was on the beach over there, and made a fire, and cooked a breakfast of fish for the disciples when they came in from fishing.

Right over there.

CHAPTER 9
The wonders of Rome

Amazing missionary adventures

The epitome of all art is in Rome. The sculptures, the huge paintings, the churches, the fountains, are all wonderful.

I left my suitcase and guitar in the Hotel room and joined the tour. My Dad had lent me his new movie camera, which had the large video cassette in it. You could just plug it into a video machine and play it.

I took the movie camera with me.

At noon, the bus driver said for everyone to just leave all of our belongings on the bus, and he would lock it up. We went to lunch and when we got back to the bus, it was a different bus. The driver said all of our belongings had been moved to this bus, and all would be well. Well, my camera was missing. He said, "don't worry, he would notify the garage, and they would locate it." At the end of the day, I got the address of the garage, and our original bus was out somewhere. It was all a scam . Some other people were also missing their things too.

The next day, we were at a Roman aqueduct, and about twenty children came to us begging. Suddenly they were all pulling on our clothing, begging, and three women lost their purses, as the children ran away very fast. They had an escape route, and we couldn't even find them. They had cut the straps of the purses and ran. I prayed with our group for protection for all of us, and for the rest of our journey, nothing else went missing.

We visited about forty churches, and not one person at a church offered us Christianity. This really bothered me. I had visited Robert Schuler's "Crystal Cathedral", in Anaheim, California, and every tour group, sat through an entire salvation meeting. People actually got saved too.

Although Rome is the epicenter of the Roman Catholic Church, they don't appear to entice tourists to Christianity.

Apparently, about ten million tourists visit every year.

(Except not now, during Covid-19)

CHAPTER 10
Kelowna to California

Amazing missionary adventures

It was good to be back home again.

I immediately got involved in my parents "Bible study", and I knew the Lord was in on it, because at the first meeting that I attended, we were having results.

As I had learned from the Lord, the only purpose of a meeting, is to do God business. The purpose is never to upgrade the teaching. People always need personal help from God. And always, God brings the right people together. The steps of a righteous man are ordered by the Lord, but so also, are the people that God gathers. They are never there by accident, or coincidence.

The Holy Spirit orchestrates everything. People's needs come to a head, for their presence, at the meeting. The Holy Spirit pressures them to participate with their need. And then their faith, and desire, is sufficiently increased, to receive from the Lord what they need. All teaching must be with the "hearing of the word of God". (Romans 10:17) The hearing builds up their faith to receive. The word of God is the power. The more word of God, the more power. Jesus always said "thy faith hath made thee whole.

(St. Luke 17:19)

And we certainly saw the power. Many people got healings. Some got jobs. Some were not your good employable candidates, but they got jobs anyway.

The beginning of every meeting was their testimony of what we had prayed for, at the last meeting. God was answering prayers. And they brought their friends.

Our pastor thought I was starting a church. We had over a hundred now. After a couple of months, the Lord told me to go south again. My parents gave me their Winnebago motor home to drive to California.

I drove to the west coast, and in Surrey stopped at the upper room. "The upper room" was the penthouse of a great Hotel in Surrey. I have no idea how God had arranged that large suite, but I'm sure there is a miracle in that story as well. It was a place to pray, and Arne Bryant ran "Prayer Canada" out of that place. Arne was a man who really had a burden for revival in Canada. He started "Prayer Canada" to have Wednesday noon Prayer meetings, in every city hall across Canada. There were people praying in that room twenty four hours a day. Miracles happened in that room as well. Fred just happened to be there that afternoon. Fred was a furniture salesman who had been led to the Lord by Arne a few months earlier. Fred had also received the baptism of the Holy Spirit and on that occasion received the gift of knowledge and the gift of prophecy. This was the first time I had ever met Fred. After much prayer, Arne told me that I had to take Fred with me. Arne insisted it was from the Lord. I really didn't want to take Fred, but Arne said, "the Lord told him". So Fred and I left. Fred had to go home first, to collect some clothes and things for the trip. So around midnight, we drove across the border and headed south.

Just past Seattle, Fred suddenly said we need to go left, east. I said, "How far" and Fred said "I don't know, but the Lord is saying to go east and he'll show us." It was my first experience with Fred, and I had never seen or heard of him before. So we were headed east. We got to Spokane, when the sun came up, and drove by at least five churches. 'Thought we might be preaching in one of them. I was hungry, so we stopped and ate. Then we slept a few hours, and around five, we woke up, and went to eat again. Then we started to drive south, right out of Spokane. Within a few miles, we came to a huge Catholic Church on our right. There were no cars in the parking lot, but Fred insisted this is where the Lord had brought us. I knocked on the front door. No answer. We waited and prayed, and within two minutes, a farmer with rubber boots on, came around the building, and asked us what we were doing here. We said, "the Lord had sent us". Then he told us to go around the back, where the meeting was. And lots of cars. There were over three hundred people at a basement meeting, with the priest up front. Everyone was sitting on those grey metal folding chairs. Fred and I sat in the last row and were handed this folded paper, which was titled "Life in the Spirit Seminar". They sang a song, and then the priest asked if anyone had had a Holy Spirit experience.

The first lady had her dog run away, and she had prayed to St. Christopher, and within one day, the dog came back.

The next Lady said she had terrible headaches, and she had prayed, and it was getting less every day.

The next was a man, who said he had cramps all the time, and he had prayed, and now he hasn't had one since.

By this time Fred had had enough, and stood up, and he asked the priest if he could come to the front. Then Fred said, "do you really want to learn about the Holy Spirit." And the priest said, "well yes", and Fred said, "the man with me is a teacher, and he can tell you all, exactly how the Holy Spirit works." The priest invited me to the front, and Fred introduced me to everyone, and then went back to the last row, and sat down. As I always do, I started praying first, and then I raised my hands right up like Moses, and said, "come Holy Spirit", and everyone fell down hard. The noise was incredible. All those metal chairs smashing down, as people fell to the ground. Only the priest and I and Fred were standing. I fully expected that many would be hurt. It took quite a while, before they started to slowly get up, and straighten out the chairs. Everyone helped everyone. They had no idea what had happened. I explained it to the priest. Many had now received the Holy Spirit and were speaking in tongues. Many also received healings. The priest was amazed. After some time had past, he announced that brother Ron was now going to teach us, about the Holy spirit." We were there for two weeks.

After that we got to preach in two Spokane churches.

Then we headed south to Portland, and went through the Redwood Forests, and when we got to Redding, California, we saw a church beside the Highway. We both got the unction from the Holy Spirit to turn off Highway 5 and circled around and drove into the Church yard. The pastor was in, and we had a nice interview. The pastor invited us to their evening service. After eating at a restaurant, we went to the service.

We were both invited to sit up at the front, on the stage. We were introduced, and then Fred was asked to speak a few words. Fred had learned a few things from me by now, and he began by raising his arms above his head and he prayed, " Lord give me the right words to say, speak through my mouth."

Then he began, "there is someone here, who was in a store this afternoon, and the Lord saw what you stole." (you could have heard a pin drop). Then Fred said, " and you two are both married but not to each other, and the Lord saw you in that motel this afternoon". And Fred called out about ten other things, and people were in absolute shock. Terrified.

(I was reminded of that Johnny Cash song: "This train is bound for glory")

Then Fred said, I think the whole church should come up to the front here and kneel before the Lord and repent. They all came quickly.

Fred asked me to take over and say the prayer.

People were crying everywhere. Even the Pastor.

The Holy Spirit came down, and it was amazing.

It lasted quite a while. We ended up doing six meetings over two weeks.

They liked the teaching. They learned how the Holy Spirit operates. We were invited to come back on our return from the south.

We continued to Los Angeles.

Now, two years later (for me), Fred and I drove into Anaheim. And I knew where a target store was, and we needed some things. I was amazed that the "Target store name" was gone. I parked at the front door, and someone came out just then, and I asked, "what is this place now". Ralph Wilkerson had bought it and turned it into a ministry.

It had a chapel, and restaurant, and about a hundred small bedrooms. Ralph and I met, and he asked us to speak tonight. It was more like a testimony meeting. Ralph was taking in street people and showing them real Christian love. We helped with the ministry, and a few days later, Fred decided to stay with this ministry. I never saw Fred or Ralph again.

The next day, I drove to Santa Anna, and because it was Wednesday, and because it was almost noon, I felt led to go to the Full Gospel Businessmen's luncheon. The place was packed, and again they ushered me up to the speakers table at the front. They served me lunch first, and when I had finished my lunch, Demos Shakarian walked in with an entourage. He was actually limping and walking very slowly. They sat him down beside me, and we shook hands. Demos had a stroke last week, and his left side was drooping. His arm and left leg were almost useless. And he could hardly talk. Then it came my time to speak. I got up at the podium, and as I had learned to do, I paused, raised my arms straight up, and prayed. I asked God to send the Holy Spirit to guide me. Before I could begin speaking, God instructed me to put my hands on Demos' head. I did. Then I prayed in tongues and then pronounced Demos healed, in Jesus' name. Demos stood up and turned around and began walking all around the outer perimeter of the room. Then from the back of the room, Demos (with his low gruff voice) said, "the Lord Jesus has healed me." Everyone clapped, and it took several minutes for the room to come to order again. Demos sat down, and I was told to continue. I told several stories of things that had happened to me, and then I walked around the room, and had words of knowledge and words of wisdom and direction for several people. Then the Lord showed me several people that needed healing. A man from San Diego invited me to come speak in San Diego. A dentist came to me, and asked if I needed a Dentist, and I said yes. He gave me his card.

The next day, without an appointment, I went there, and he took me right in, and worked on several teeth. No Charge. Then I asked him why he really asked me to come to him. He had a list of home problems.

In San Diego, I began a street ministry on a corner, and met a Harvard lawyer, who invited me to his home. On the way there (in his car) he stopped at a shoe store and said he had noticed my worn out shoes and said he would like to buy me new one's.

The dinner was great, and I prayed for his family. The next day, He took me to his office. He was a very eloquent black lawyer, with an awesome office on the twentieth floor. He wrote me a cheque as well. He also gave me the address of a pastor he knew. I got to preach in an all black church in El Cajon. What an experience. Their enthusiasm, and their singing, and their love of God, was amazing. God sent me there to learn.

I continued with the street ministry and met another street minister named Harry. He said he knew many good people and introduced me to another lawyer.

Harry also took me to a hostel, where I ministered.

Then I decided to go back home.

Before Sacramento, very early in the morning, I was driving the motorhome, when suddenly I had the most horrible toothache. It was excruciating pain and it blinded me for the moment. It went up into my brain and I couldn't believe how much pain I had. Then I remembered who I was, and I yelled out "get away from me devil, I belong to Jesus." The pain went away immediately. I was glad that there were no cars around me. I could easily have had an accident. A few minutes later it happened again. This time I rebuked the devil and asked God to bind the strongman and the devil and send them to the pit.

The pain stopped and I knew it was just an attack, a test that God had allowed. I was learning.

In Sacramento, I went into a Macy's store, and almost immediately met an East Indian man, who was also shopping. He was there with his family, and he asked me something, and we started to talk. Turned out he was a pastor who had a church. His family was from Fiji. He invited me, and I spent a whole week with his church. Before I left, he said he still had friends in Fiji, and a young pastor had just died in a car accident, and he felt I should go to Fiji, to minister to them.

On the way north, near Clear Lake, suddenly the motorhome broke down. I managed to get off Highway 5, to the side of the highway, and was grateful to God, that I had not had an accident. I also knew immediately that this was of the Lord.

I had learned by now, that there are no coincidences. So there I was on the side of the highway, with a broken down motor home. I just prayed. There was no town nearby. No repair garage, and I knew nothing of mechanical work.

But God had a plan. He always does. (the steps of a good man are ordered by the Lord: and he delighteth in his way. Though he fall, he shall not be utterly cast down: for the Lord upholdeth him with his hand. (Psalms 37:23-24) I knew that.

It took a while and finally, an old pickup truck stopped, and an unruly looking man came to the side door and asked "what was wrong." "I said, "I don't know". He crawled under the motor home and in a few minutes told me the transmission had broken. He said I'll be back.

And he left.

An hour later, he came with a tow truck and pulled the motorhome many miles, to the top of a mountain at Clear Lake. His house was half buried in the top of this mountain, to cope with the strong winds. He also had a mechanical building and worked on the motorhome for three days. Every night he would come into the motor home and teach me what he knew of the Bible. He taught me the entire teaching on the fire that shall devour before him. (2 Thessalonians 1: 7-10)

He never charged me for the entire repair.

He took me to his church on Sunday. A Pentecostal Holiness Church. I taught there for a week. Then I drove north to the Pentecostal Holiness Church in Redding and taught there again.

Then I drove all the way to Bellingham and stopped to phone the man I had met in Amman, Jordan. He invited me to do a Bible study at their home that night, but since it was early, I drove to Surrey, B.C., to visit my friend, Arne Bryant, at the upper room. Arne talked me into starting a prayer Canada Chapter, with the mayor of Kelowna, in the City Hall in Kelowna.

Eventually I headed back south on King George Highway, to go back to the US border, and I needed gas.

I stopped on King George Highway, and while I was gassing up, a car drove up beside me, and three fellows and a girl got out. We started talking, and they asked me what I did, and I said I was headed to a Bible study in Lynden, Washington. They said that was really odd, because they had just been debating Christianity amongst each other, and since their lives weren't going very well, they wondered if there really was a God. I invited them to come with me, and we found a place to park their car, and we drove to Lynden. They were in the drug business, but that wasn't going so well. I told them a bit of what I had done. In Lynden, they got saved within half an hour. Then I began to teach seriously. They ended up going to this bible study for years. I baptized them in the ocean at White Rock, B.C.

In Kelowna, I started teaching again.

And I did start that Kelowna "Prayer Canada" chapter, in the City Hall, every Wednesday noon. It amazed me, how many of the council attended, and they brought there staff too.

My mothers cooking was far beyond amazing. And there were always other people there, to enjoy Mom's hospitality. After church on Sunday, five couples would come over, and fellowship for the rest of the day. I'd pull out my guitar, and we would all sing gospel songs. My Mom and Dad collected Gaither music video's. When they were alone, they would sit in their two recliner chairs, and watch the Gaither's on their TV. The songs were very moving, and often I would catch them with tears in their eyes, hearing the lovely words about heaven. In their travels, with their motor home, they had actually met many of the singers.

We often talked about the TV evangelists too.

I loved Jimmy Swaggart's music. They actually knew most of the evangelists.

When these evangelists started to fall off, because of sin, the entire Christian community around North America, had nothing but distain for them. Somehow Christians think they personally, are above sin. That they are immune to temptation. That forgiveness isn't their responsibility. That looking down on other people's sinful stain, is showing, that they are so much better.

Every Christian has an area in their life, that the devil tempts them in. It is the weakness, that every Christian has. The sin which doth so easily beset us. (Hebrews 12:1)

And the greater the ministry of a saint is, the stronger the temptation is, in that area.

I've met great preachers all over the world. Some of them you probably have heard of. And if I told you some of the things I saw, and experienced in great disappointment, you would be shocked. King Jesus told us how to react to these things.

Judge not, that ye be not judged. (Matthew 7:1-3)

I have many Bible heroes. I have studied them thoroughly.
King Solomon had so much wisdom. God gave him that special gift.
Other Kings came from their countries, just to listen to Solomon.
Solomon wrote:
Forsake the foolish and live. And go in the way of understanding.
(that is so profound and yet it is so simple.)
He that reproveth a scorner,
getteth to himself shame:

And he that rebuketh a wicked man
getteth himself a blot. (what a great lesson)
Reprove not a scorner, lest he hate thee:
Rebuke a wise man, and he will love thee.
Give instruction to a wise man,
and he will be yet wiser:
teach a just man,
and he will increase in learning. (Proverbs 9: 6-9)
King Solomon also said:
By mercy and truth, iniquity is purged:
and by fear of the Lord, men depart from evil.
(I teach that, as a parenting lesson)

When a man's ways please the Lord,
He maketh even his enemies
to be at peace with him. (Proverbs 16:6-7)

CHAPTER 11
Hawaii to Fiji

Amazing missionary adventures

The Lord had spoken to me, to go to India.

I was hoping it was Indiana. I never had an East Indian friend, so I knew almost nothing about India.

I never asked anyone for money, but I did hand out my parent's address, and phone number, in case anyone needed me.

God motivated people to send cheques to my parents, and they started a tax company, called "Son Life Ministries". My Parents invited and prepared a board of directors, with no other purpose, than to keep me on the road, preaching the Kingdom of God, and healing the sick.

I was sitting on the plane, on the left side, beside the window, and we had reached our altitude, and were soon around Seattle, when suddenly the pilot came on the air and said, "Mount St. Helens is just now erupting and if you look out of the left side, you can see it. He also said to take turns coming from the right side, as to not shift the plane. I had just been praying about India, and asked God, "is this trip really from you. Do you really want me to end up in India?"

I looked out of the window, and there was a huge, perfect cross, on top of the mountain. The volcanic ash shooting straight up, eventually starting to come back down because of gravity, and then spreading out in arms because the stuff going up was hitting the ash coming down and the arms made a perfect cross. It was astounding. I was crying. That God had gone to all that trouble just for me. Wow.

God had told me to buy a round trip ticket (round the world) and I flew from Vancouver to Hawaii. I got involved immediately, with people I just randomly met. We had home Bible studies, and it was great. Some on the beach, where tourists could join in. I even got to go to a "Full Businessmen's Convention", and the man who invited me, paid for me. The teaching and testimonies were great. It was refreshing.

Then I decided to fast and pray. I had not done that for a long time.

Then I left for Fiji. Still had the address, where the young pastor had died in a car crash. I didn't go there right away. In Nadi (pronounced Nandi) I lived in a cheap motel and just started walking. A man on a motorcycle stopped beside me and asked what I was doing in Nadi. Turned out, he had a small church beside the river, and invited me to preach on Sunday with an interpreter. His name was David Krishna.

I was thrilled that God was working with me so fast.

Next day David came to my motel and asked if I could go to a bible study up in the hills. I sat on the back of this motorcycle, and it was precarious. Dirt road most of the way, and we finally arrived at the home of David Ram Shandra. The Bible study went fine, but the main reason I was there, was to pray for Davids wife who was very sick. I did, and then God showed me why she wasn't getting well. Her husband was a fervent Christian, but she was still involved with her parent's Hindu religion. I told her, if she would break away from her Hindu religion, God would heal her. She refused.

I found out she also had two idols. When I left, she was still sick. I went back twice more, over the next few months. The last time, she died.

I was really disappointed.

I taught at a church in Nadi near the airport corners, with a great group of pastors. The church was just poles and a corrugated tin roof. And wooden planks on stumps as benches. One night after a meeting, which lasted almost until midnight, they announced that I should go with them to Suva. Suva is on the other side of the island. They said they were all going to a pastors meeting. They had an old Datsun car, and these men were big men. Two in the front and another fellow and me in the back. I sat on the right side. Fijians have a tendency to drive really fast. It shows their skill. They had tied my suitcase and my guitar on the roof along with their huge blanket of stuff. We left after midnight. At that time the roads in Fiji were all made of crushed coral because they had no stone or gravel. It was very sharp on the tires. The drive to Suva is mostly on the side of a mountain and there is about a twenty feet drop on the right side. After about an hour, there was suddenly a very loud bang under my seat, and we stopped the car, and we all got out, to look at what had happened. All of the tread had come off the tire under my seat. The tire was still inflated, but it only had threads now. I said, "thank you God, that we didn't have an accident." OK, lets change the tire. Then they told me that they didn't have a spare tire. There were no shops anywhere until we got to Suva, so they decided to drive on these threads all the way to Suva. Another couple of hours. I knelt down beside the tire and prayed that God would protect this tire all the way. And he did. The driver didn't even slow down.

We had a great meeting in Suva. And I met some other pastors. Pastor John from eight miles, (that's a place) invited me to preach. His church was kind of on stilts. But a great group of people. I worked with them several times.

One day, we had a baptism out in the forest. The trees were kind of what you would see in a Tarzan movie, with long vines that you could swing on from tree to tree.

I also got to minister to some Methodists priests in the farmers market Suva. They had lost their salvation thrust entirely. This farmers market was at the bottom of the hill in Suva, and I would talk to people in the market, whenever I was down there.

One day, I was taken early in the morning to an AOG Bible school, in Navua. The place was run by Americans, and was really a work of art. Beautiful, like an expensive resort. They had a large auditorium, and all of the students had been told to attend. I was the visiting speaker. They sang a couple of songs, and then the Professor invited me to speak. Once on stage, I did what I usually do. I hesitated. Then lifted my hands straight up, and prayed to God, to give me the Holy Spirit, for direction and guidance. Then God showed me what was wrong. Most of the students were very sick.

I raised my hands again and prayed and God told me what to do. I invited them all to the front. The professors didn't know what I saw. I told them. Then I asked the students to raise their hands, if they were really sick. They did. I went down the lines and quickly touched each one of them on the forehead. Some collapsed. When they recovered, I asked if anyone felt that they were still sick, and God had healed them all. Then I taught about the gifts of the Holy Spirit, and many of them received gifts.

I went back to Nadi, and immediately got involved again. Mostly home Bible studies.

I also found the address of the pastor, who had died in a car crash, and went to that place in Ba.

James was the father in law, and he invited me to stay with them. It was a nice house. James was a builder. His wife was a great cook. The daughter, who was the wife of the young preacher that had died, was extremely depressed. She thought her life was over. She had such high hopes, because her husband had been very popular, and now it was all gone. I stayed with them for some weeks. The Bible studies went well. Then one Sunday, the daughter wouldn't go to Church. I was asked to stay with her. They went to church. The daughter was in her room, and I stayed in mine. It was a set up. They were hoping that there would be an attraction by me, to the daughter. When they came home and realized that nothing had happened, the daughter became very irritated. She left the house, and we didn't find her, for over a week. Turned out she had moved in with a taxi driver, and she wouldn't come home.

One day I was asked to go to the Hospital in Lautoka. I prayed for many patients there. Then I was told the real reason they had wanted me to come there. This hospital had five floors, but they only used the first three. The top two floors were full of demons. When anyone went up there, the furniture started moving around, and there was much metal banging and things flying in the air.

No one would dare go up there anymore.

The manager of the Hospital would not let me go up to the top. It was an insurance matter. It wasn't safe, and I wasn't staff or on contract. I did pray from the first floor. Nothing changed. I left, wondering what I could have done.

Years later I asked my mechanic, who was from Lautoka, and he said it was still like that.

Eventually I moved to Suva. I found a place at the top of the hill at "eight miles". There was an AOG church at the corner, and next to it, was the Tanoa house. This became my base.

I got involved with Pastor Johns church and enjoyed being in Fiji.

CHAPTER 12
Tonga
(The first time)

Amazing missionary adventures

The town of Suva was quaint. Much of Suva was still very old fashioned, like it had been 80 years ago. I was walking near the waterfront early one morning, when a man in a blue suit stopped me, and asked where I was from. I told him, and he said that I should go to Tonga. I asked him where Tonga was, and he told me. Then, while I was standing there, he disappeared. I was in shock. Right out of the blue, a man says I should go to Tonga. I checked it out, and Tonga was 550 miles southeast of Fiji. The only way there, was by plane. I went back to Nadi and arranged my ticket and flew to Tonga.

I knew it was from God.

Tonga had a runway for the Jet, and a customs building that looked more like a mobile home.

I was the only passenger, and once I got my passport stamped, there was a waiting room, like at a bus depot, with a wooden bench. I went outside, and there was a mile long gravel driveway (actually it was coral, not gravel), and palm tree fields on both sides. No taxies and no people. Suddenly an old Datsun car came down this road, and stopped right in front of me, and a tall silver haired man jumped out, and went right into the airport. He acted like I wasn't there. Then he came out and said, "who are you".

I explained myself, and he said jump in, I'll give you a ride. He said his name was Peter. On the way, he asked where I was staying, and I had no idea. He said he knew of a guest house, and he dropped me off there. A lovely Tongan lady greeted me and showed me to my room . It was about ten feet long and eight feet wide, and very clean and tidy. I sat on the bed and prayed and said "God, why did you send me here?" God just said, "you'll see".

I went to the living room, where about twenty people were sitting around, mostly reading. It was just before supper time.

The Tongan lady brought out fruit, and a Taro soup, which was delicious. The people there all looked like hippies, with very tropical clothing, and longish hair.

They asked me where I was from, and what I did.

I realized God was opening a door. So I told them.

I also told them some stories of miracles that had

happened to me. Then I asked them what they did.

Turned out, every one of them was a Doctor, from various countries. They were all here, to study tropical medicines. Now they started to ask me more specific questions, about healings and miracles. I was right into it. I explained what I had learned so far, and they said that during the day, they all worked at the Vaiola Hospital.

They invited me to come and work at the Vaiola Hospital and perhaps some patients would get healed too. The next day was Saturday, and I said I would go to the hospital on Monday. Breakfast was great. The lady served a very large bowl of soup, that was amazing. I couldn't believe how good it tasted. I asked what was in it, and they explained that it was fish cut up in fruit juices. I asked how they cook it, and they said it is not cooked. It is just marinated over night. There was a type of bread, and instead of butter, they used avocado. Tonga doesn't have cattle, so butter was not available. Perhaps now they do, but at that time they didn't. The avocado on bread is really good.

After breakfast, I used the shower, and then I went for a walk. After about a mile, I saw a fairly nice home that looked like it was foreign. Most houses at that time were straw and thatched roofs. The guest house I was in was wooden, and very simple. Just two by fours and wood on the outside. No Gyproc anywhere.

This foreign looking house attracted me, and when I came closer, a man ran out toward me, and stopped in front of me, and asked where I was from.

I told him I was from Canada, and that I was here to teach about Jesus. He immediately asked, "what do you know about the Holy Spirit?" And I told him that I was baptized by the Holy Spirit, and I speak in tongues and occasionally I prophesy. He said, "You need to come into my house and meet my wife. We have a story to tell you." I went in and met the wife.

They were both Tongan and spoke perfect English.

They were both educated in England. Last night they had both been praying before they went to bed. He had prayed, that God would show him what to do about the Holy Spirit. He was the Anglican Priest here in Tonga, and he had received letters from overseas, that there was a movement of the Holy Spirit, and everyone was very concerned about it.

So he was asking God what to do about it, and God baptized both of them with the Holy Spirit, and they had both started speaking in tongues, and didn't know what it was all about. You can imagine how relieved they were when I started to explain it all. God had sent a minister from Canada, at the same time that they had received the baptism of the Holy Spirit. We were instant friends. Turned out that not only did he have a church, but also a school of 1500 children.

And the headmaster of that school was none other than the man that had picked me up at the airport. Peter Chignell and I became friends, and he invited me to teach at the school. I was given half an hour every morning, with the entire student body. Then I had one hour music classes every day.

I usually taught until noon. Then I would rush to the Vaiola Hospital, to teach in their large lunchroom.

It was a long room, with a table the full length of the room. The Nurses all had lovely blue uniforms. The doctors wore white. We would pray, and then I would teach. Usually they had people for me to pray for, at the end. It was usually a time of miracles. God was answering my prayers.

One day they had a demon possessed man they wanted to show me. I don't know why they had not shown him to me before. Probably, it was because they thought that he was beyond hope.

This man was about 45 and huge. All Tongan men are large, but this one was exceptional. They were all terrified of him. Things were passed through an opening in the door. Even that was scary for them.

And he had been there for several years. I prayed outside, and asked God what I should do. God said go in and lay your hands on him. Wow. OK. So I told them that I was going in. They said I shouldn't go in because this man was far too dangerous. I said, "Not for God. God won't let me be harmed". I immediately thought about Shadrach, Meshach, and Abednego in Nebuchadnezzar's fiery furnace. If they weren't afraid, why should I be afraid now. We had the same God. They carefully opened the door, and quickly shut it behind me. The possessed man just looked at me, and I think he was afraid of me. Then he started acting really crazy, with flaying of his arms and grunting and then yelling in the Tongan language, and then he came toward me. I put up my arms and said , "in the name of Jesus be still". He stopped and then I started praying in tongues. I went toward him and gestured for him to kneel down. He did. Then I continued in tongues, and after a very short time demons came out of him, yelling at me. I could hear them all around me, trying to scare me at first, and then begging me to let them stay. I continued in tongues, and then in English. I commanded them to leave Tonga and go straight to the pit. You could hear them leave. The man was now laying on the floor. He had been bouncing around, while the demons had been coming out. I knew what to expect, so, I was not afraid. He was bleeding now, from several places, because this cell was steel, and sharp braces on the walls. Then he was crying, and I went and held him. I got some blood on me too. But he was changed now. Eventually I went to the door and told them to come in now. They treated his wounds and reassigned him to a better room. Before he left, I asked them to interpret, and I led this man to the Lord. He actually prayed his own prayer.

They were amazed, and so was I. They wanted to observe him for a few days, which they did.

God had given me an interpreter, who was also a great musician. Havili Sefesi had a small band of three other boys, who were all very talented. But Havili was really exceptional. He played guitar beautifully, and he can also play piano. Havili played the music at all of my meetings.

Havili Sefesi is second from the left

Even back then, Havili was very anointed, and sang in such a way, that the entire audience would weep. His genuine love for God was unusual. Worshipping God, and praising King Jesus, brings the Holy Spirit upon us, before we receive the message of preaching. (like Psalms 95 and 96)

I also visited people in villages quite far from Nuku Alofa.

There was a family in one village, that had a wooden house with two rooms. They wanted me to sleep in the only bed they owned. Reluctantly, I did, and it was really a good bed. I woke up in the morning and my arm was very swollen. And it really hurt.

The lady of the house looked at it and knew right away what had caused it. She said a spider had bitten me. We looked for the spider, and there it was, under the blanket . Big as my hand and furry brown. They rushed me to the Vaiola Hospital, and it turned out, no one knew what to do. They said they would fly me to Fiji. I must have passed out.

I woke up in the hospital near Suva and found out they did not have a cure either. I was running a very high fever and my arm was huge. Someone said they had called a special lady to come and help me. Soon she was there, and she was mixing some sort of drink, from the things she had brought.

She had me sit up and drink it. She said drink it all fast. I did. It was horrible. Tasted like gasoline. Later I found out, it was mostly ginger and spices and chili peppers. It worked, and after a couple of weeks, I was on my way back to Tonga. Yes, I wondered why, this had happened to me. 'Never did find out who paid for the airfare to Fiji. Or back to Tonga. 'Never did find out who the old Fijian lady was, that made the drink. God did so many miracles. And he saved me once again.

About a month later, Peter Chignell invited me to stay with him for free. He had a three bedroom home and lived there by himself. Again, God had sent a blessing.

One day, Peter suggested that we take a jungle walk. There was a forest along the ocean, and we entered from the beach. This was a dead forest.

Every tree was dead. When the tide was in, there was about six inches of water in the forest. Unfortunately, it was salt water, which killed all plantation. We walked a long way into the forest, and then we prayed. God showed me that the earth is soon doomed, and the gospel must be spread.

Peter was a professor, that was a constant source of information that was always fascinating.

Ron Preaching in a Tongan Church with an interpreter

I had meetings every night downtown, at the park, and people were being taught about water baptism this week. There were about 125,000 people in Tonga, and we had huge baptisms, mostly in the river.

One week they invited me to a cookout, and we would then also have a baptism. Everyone was carrying food things, and we went into a very heavy jungle area. After several miles, we came to the ocean, in the most beautiful spot in the whole world. A large horse-shoe beach with very white sand and clear blue, very warm water. They made food, and I prepared the baptism people. I made sure they understood, what we were doing this for. Then I invited everyone to the beach to participate. People were all around the horseshoe watching, as one by one, we baptized them.

My interpreter was standing on the other side of the person being baptized, and together we would dunk them backwards, under the four feet of water. Then it happened. We were waiting for the next person to arrive, and suddenly, without warning, the man beside me had his long machete in the air and swiftly shot it down, right beside my bare foot. He brought the sword-like machete up, and had a 20 inch fish stuck on the end of it. Then he explained. That fish had buried itself in the sand and was completely camouflaged in the sand. This fish actually looked like sand, when out of the water.

But the Lord had showed this man a slight movement of sand, down in the water, and he struck swiftly. This fish has very poisonous spikes on his back.

Later we had the dinner that was being prepared.

They had a young pig on a spit above the fire.

They had placed stones that they had heated in the fire, in a hole that they had dug in the sand, and then wrapped taro and other vegetables in banana leaves and placed them on the stones and covered the hole with sand. It was the most delicious meal. The meat from the young pig was incredible.

Peter Chignell's house was sitting on wooden blocks about a foot high. The sinks and bathtub drain into pipes, that let water down onto the sand below the house. About three o'clock in the morning, I was woken with this terrible banging in the bathroom. Peter had gone in there, and noticed a scorpion in the bathtub, and got his machete, and killed the scorpion in the tub. It had crawled up the drainpipe.

My Mother would have been upset now, at the scratched up bathtub.

On another occasion, I was at a midnight funeral for a lady that had died. She was buried above the sand, and they built the sand up about four feet. They placed large bottles all around her burial, and then we sang and prayed. During all this, a teenage girl got bit buy a scorpion. There was screaming, and I ran over to her, and began to pray. I claimed her healed in Jesus' name. She was healed instantly. She could have died.

I was getting to like my ritual with the school, and the hospital and the evening sessions. One night we had a great healing session at the end of the teaching. Many were healed. Then they brought a lady to me that was blind. She had been blind for many years. An educated lady. I did everything the same, and nothing happened. I prayed in tongues; I prayed in English. I asked God what to do. He said you can stop. I did. We both went home disappointed.

The next morning, a Colonel from the Army knocked on our door. He said the King has summoned me. (If the King summons you, it is a criminal offence to refuse the King).

He asked me if I had any military training, and I said I had been in the Royal Canadian Airforce. He said we are going to march into the Palace throne room. You will do a military stop with me. And we will stand at attention. You will not speak unless the King asks you a question. Then you will answer with only one sentence, and if the King wants to hear more, he will say so. You will begin every sentence, with: "your Majesty". Do you have a suit and tie? I said yes.

He said he would be back to pick me up, and he left.

I dressed and sat ready to leave. I wondered why the King had summoned me. I sat the whole day, and nothing happened. I was wondering what the delay was, and I prayed. God said to be anxious for nothing. The next morning, I was ready to go again. Nothing happened all day. And no one came to make an excuse. Peter said not to worry. God is in control.

I should tell you, that while I was waiting, all I did was read my Bible and pray. Mostly pray. In English and in tongues.

The third morning, the Colonel came to pick me up, and said that some ambassadors had arrived, and the King was busy. We marched into the throne room and stood at attention. The King was on his throne. Beside him was Queen Salote. Beside her, was Princess Malanite and her husband, the Prime minister, (who was also the brother of the King). The royal family was there. The Honor Guard, with machine guns were there. The visiting ambassadors were there, a Lady from Australia and an ambassador (man) from Thailand.

Then the King spoke to me, and said "Reverend Peters, we understand that you do miracles. Last night, the Police Chiefs wife, who has been blind for many years, is now able to see, with both eyes. Can you tell us, how you do these miracles?

I was shocked.

I had no idea that she was the Police chief's wife, and I had no idea that she had been healed. I responded to the King, "your Majesty, King Jesus does the healings."

The king said, "yes, I know, but you obviously know how to entreat Jesus, to do these miracles. Could you teach my Bishops how to do this?

I responded, "Your Majesty, with their permission,

I would be greatly honored to teach your Bishops."

The King said, "I shall look forward to hearing of your success with my Bishops".

The King asked me if I had any questions. (I thought this was a very odd thing, for the King to ask me. Then I realized that it was the Lord God).

I spoke boldly, and said, "Your Majesty, I have a personal message for you, from the Lord"

The King said, "Alright"

To which I said, "Your Majesty, I will need to come to you, and put my hands on your head, when I deliver this message."

The King beckoned me with his hands.

The moment I moved, I heard all this clicking of the loading of the machine guns. The Colonel put his hands in the air and slowly brought them down. The guns came down too. I went up onto the stage, and was totally surprised when the King stood up, and knelt down. It was hard for him. He was over four hundred pounds. I said to him, "would you rather we do this in some private room, and he said "no, this will be fine."

I started to say, "the Spirit of the Lord is upon me, Thus saith the Lord:

"You remember on the day of your Coronation, when you went out into the garden, behind the palace, and you promised to maintain the nation of Tonga in Holiness and righteousness, and you asked me to continue the blessing in Tonga, above all other nations.

I have continued the blessing on the Nation of Tonga, but your people have back slidden, and have not listened to your call for righteousness. If you do not bring your nation back into Holiness, I will remove the blessing, thus saith the Lord."

The king was weeping very hard, and Queen Salote, brought tissues to the King, and he continued to weep.

Everyone had heard the message, and the room was in total silence, except for the King.

Eventually the King stood up, and looked at me, and said, "Thankyou for the message from the Lord"

Then he dismissed me, and the Colonel and I marched out of the building.

I was in awe of the Lord. He had always told me he would fill my mouth, but I didn't expect it to be so profound. After the Colonel drove me home, I knelt beside my bed, and thanked the Lord for his greatness.

I did get to meet with the Methodist Bishops. They hesitated to receive the Holy Spirit Baptism. They couldn't see how they could remain Methodist's with this Pentecostal teaching. I told them, that the gift of healing is only by the Holy Spirit, and that the Baptism was a prerequisite. They said they would all think about it and let me know. They never did.

I did get to preach in a Methodist church. It was over 80 degrees outside. So I walked in with my short sleeved white shirt, and tie, and was immediately ushered out of the church by a man at the door. Outside, he was polite, and told me that I was improperly dressed. When John Wesley brought Christianity to Tonga, he wore a black suit, a white shirt, and a black tie . This is still the proper dress to go into church. Of course they are barefoot because they don't have leather. John's wife wore a black dress, to the ground, with long sleeves, and an apron. Tongan women still dress like that, but the apron is made out of basket weave. So the man who took me out of the church, took off his suit jacket, and gave it to me, so that I could go in. Of course he had to stay outside during the service.

The pulpit in a Methodist church is quite high, and they have steps going up in a circular fashion, to the top landing. Before I started, I had to give them all my scripture references. What I did not realize, is that they had a man read all of these scriptures from the pulpit, before I started.

For me, it spoiled my lesson.

Soon, things turned to normal.

I stayed a few more weeks, and then the Lord said to go to New Zealand.

CHAPTER 13
New Zealand

Amazing missionary adventures

I flew to Auckland, and again I was totally lost.

I knew nobody and had no plan. It was a shock, to suddenly be in a modern city again, with restaurants and office buildings, and all the trappings. I remember how it all started in New Zealand. I met someone in a Bible store, who invited me to their church bible study that night. From there, God opened the doors in 72 places. And people had me stay in their homes, and I was busy every single day.

I preached in the following cities:
New Plymouth - twice
Auckland - many times
Christ Church - in several places
Timaru
Ruakak in Northland
Opunake - twice
Kawerau - for two weeks
Palmerston North - with two churches
Greymouth for two weeks
Blenheim
Pakuranga
Nelson - for a week
Levin

Feilding
Opotiki
Devonport
Mairangi Bay
Rotorua - for a week
Whagerei
Whakatane
Eketahuna -twice
Tauranga - twice
Epsom

I baptized people in many places and God was always present.

In Christ Church, I was asked if I could do an afternoon session at a person's place. I expected a mature group of adults. Instead I was shown a group of children, all under ten, and the room was in a large car garage.

Believe it or not, I had a great time with the children. I really enjoyed them. And I learned a lot. Their questions were sometimes funny, sometimes very personal, and some well thought out. Some out of confusion. But what they liked, was that it was God stuff. As if God was right there, answering their young minds. And I loved it. God did say he would give me the right words to say.

There were a couple of Mill towns, like Rotorua and Kawerau and Whagerei. These towns smelled like sulfur. One thing I enjoyed, is that the places were volcanic. Which meant the water in the ditches was really warm. And I swam in one of those warm ditches.

It was great.

New Zealand had some very modern farms. One couple I stayed with, showed me their dairy farm.

The cows would line up properly, to be milked. Then they would, by themselves, climb onto a very large circular merry go round, in orderly fashion, as a stall would become available, because a cow had just left.

Once on this circular ramp, the cows would get a car wash, from sprayers, milkers would be attached, they would get high quality hay and chop, and water, and all this time, they would be listening to very fine classical music. The cows loved it. And they were very good producers.

I also got invited to do a radio show, and I enjoyed it.

I also spoke at several Full Gospel Businessmen's Dinners.

Then I flew to Sydney Australia.

CHAPTER 14
Sydney Australia

Amazing missionary adventures

Australia is nothing like New Zealand.

The people aren't open and friendly like New Zealand.

Some are, but most aren't.

Walking the streets, I found a church that was large inside, but had a street entrance, that did not resemble a church. I met with the pastor, and he invited me to their next meeting. I went, but was never asked to the front, or, to in anyway participate. I never went back.

I found a fellow who was from a church on the other side of town. A long taxi ride. But I was immediately asked to say a few words after I was introduced, and following that, I was asked to do the evening service, and then the Wednesday night service. And I stayed in one of their homes too.

CHAPTER 15
Singapore

Amazing missionary adventures

The Lord told me to move on, and I booked a trip to Singapore. I stayed in a downtown Hotel. I think it was the Mandarin. The Airport was very modern, but the plane stayed quite far from the airport, and when we walked out of the plane, down the stairs, there were bus trains available, to take us to the main airport terminal. These buses were side loading, and the entire side, three busses long, opened for us to walk in. Very efficient.

Customs was fast. The taxi driver I had, had this very small car, and drove scary fast. I asked him to take me to a downtown Hotel. The Mandarin Hotel was fine, and after checking in, and leaving my cases in the room, I was on an elevator, which somehow I had pressed the wrong button. We were going up instead of down. The other man in this elevator asked if I was going to the meeting, because I had traveled in a suit. I said, what kind of meeting. He said, "Full Gospel Businessmen's meeting, on the very top floor". I said no, but I would love to go. He asked where I was from, and what I did. Then he said he would pay for my lunch. At the luncheon, several men made it a point to screen me. Then I was asked to say a few words to the large gathering of over a hundred men, in this rooftop restaurant. I spoke and then they asked me to be the main speaker today. I was told, I had half an hour. After half an hour they asked me to continue, and I began to tell them of some of my travel experiences. They loved it. After the meeting, I was invited to several other places. God had placed me in the right Hotel, on the right elevator, going the wrong way, and opened the doors in Singapore.

Rev. Randy Sing also opened more doors for me.

I had planned to go to Kuala Lumpur, in Malaysia, but the Lord told me to book the next trip straight to Calcutta, (now called Kolkata) West Bengal, India.

CHAPTER 16
Bangkok

Amazing missionary adventures

The Airbus I was on, was huge. And I'm not positive, but I may have been the only white person on this plane. We were headed for Calcutta.

I sat near the middle of the plane. Then suddenly we were in a horrible storm. The pilot said they were looking for a way around it, and we should be prepared for much turbulence. The plane was dropping and climbing, and it was rough. Then something happened which terrified everyone. Lightning hit our plane, and this very bright blue light flew through the entire length of this large plane. The pilot came on and said that there was nothing to be afraid of, that the lightning would not do any damage.

Meanwhile because of the storm and high winds, the plane inside, was weaving side to side like a snake, from front to back. The 747's never do that. But the Airbus planes are different. And apparently they can take that kind of metal fatigue.

Because of the storm, we couldn't make it to Calcutta. We landed in Bangkok, Thailand. About twenty huge planes had already landed there. The airport at that time had a low 10 foot ceiling and thousands of people were already sleeping on the floors. Eventually I found a place for my guitar and suitcase and sort of laid on top of them for security and tried to sleep. The entire airport had this body odor. And children were crying. About 30 hours later we finally boarded for Calcutta.

CHAPTER 17
Calcutta

Amazing missionary adventures

The old airport in Calcutta had huge lineups. My estimate would be around ten thousand people. Again, a low ceiling. Eventually I got to get my luggage. The strange part was, they didn't have a carousel, but long straight old conveyer rollers. And on top of my suitcase was a large live rat. Just a bit unusual.

At least 35 Jumbo Jets had landed in Calcutta since the storm had delayed them all. I stood at the end of a almost ten thousand person lineup and because I was tired, and hungry, (there was no food in Bangkok)

I prayed that the Lord would help me make it through this line-up. I recalled my experience in Los Angeles when he told me to go to Motel Six.

It happened that I had been wearing a nice American suit, that I had been gifted. Just like that, a Major in the Army walked right up to me in his fancy uniform, saluted me, and said, "Sir, please follow me. I never even had to get my passport checked at customs. He walked me right out of the Airport, to a waiting Limousine. The Major opened my door and asked the driver to take me to my hotel. And off we went. A short way out of the airport, there was a long dead snake in the middle of the road, and I asked the driver why no one had removed it. He said, in India, no one will ever touch a snake. Snakes always travel in tribes, and if one of them is killed, the others go and smell it, and although it may take time, if a human has touched it, the tribe will find you and kill you. I asked the driver to take me to a downtown hotel, which he did. He carried my luggage into the Hotel, I tipped him, and he left. I had no intention of staying in this expensive hotel, and I immediately asked the concierge to get me a taxi. They loaded my luggage, and I directed the cab driver to take me to Mark Buntain's place. He said he knew where it was.

I had seen Mark Buntain on Television, and it was the only name I knew in India. It looked like a four story red brick factory or warehouse building. The taxi left, and it took some time, and finally the men led me up to the fourth floor of this building. Apparently, Mark and his wife had the entire top floor of this large building. Mark's wife came out and asked why I was here, and I told her who I was, and she said, I could wait inside. It wasn't really inside. They had a sort of veranda all around their home with wicker furniture and small wicker tables for drinks. The furniture had colored padded pillows which made very comfortable sitting. About an hour later, Mark came home, and interviewed me. Then He said he would now arrange for me to stay at the Bengal Chambers downtown. He said not to leave the Bengal Chambers for any reason, that it was far to dangerous. I was to stay in my room, until he would come and instruct me further. He seemed upset that I was even there. I had hoped that there would be some kind of place for me, helping his organization.

That never came up for discussion.

A taxi was waiting for me.

In my room at the Bengal Chambers, I got on my knees and began to pray. I thanked the Lord for bringing me here safely. I thanked him for the miracle at the Airport. Then I asked the Lord, if he really brought me to India, to sit in a room. Immediately, God said to go out for a long walk. I had a meal before I left, and the food wasn't bad. It certainly wasn't American, but it was alright.

Then I walked.

What I had not even heard about, was that Bangladesh had a civil war, and well over two million people had fled that war, and come to Calcutta without anything. No suitcases, no money, and no passports.

Only their families.

Calcutta was built by the British for about a million people. Calcutta had now grown to over ten million people. So it was already in huge trouble before the Bangladesh people arrived. I was told at that time, that about two and half million Bangladesh refugees had arrived into Calcutta.

And because they had no money, about twenty-five hundred a day were dying of diseases and malnutrition. The Russian Communist party was the government of West Bengal. The Russians were disgusted with all the awful dead bodies, and the thousands of people that were in the throws of dying. So the Russians went to Mother Theresa and asked her to build a place for these people to die. She had no land, so the Russians brought in some heavy equipment, and bulldozed down a Hindu burial ground, and put up a large two story building, to house the dying. It was to be a place to die with dignity. They named that place Kalighat.

So, now, this was my first day in Calcutta, and as I was walking, I found so many people dying. People were laying on the sidewalks everywhere.

After a couple of miles I found a large pink church. The sign said they were Baptists. I knocked on the door and asked for the Pastor. It took time, but he came out and invited me in. We had chai, and he asked me to speak at their meeting tonight. That was the start. This Pastor had me teach at night meetings and he also knew many other pastors around the city. I went to a morning pastors meeting with him, and that really opened the doors. It also opened my eyes to what was really going on in this city. They needed teaching badly. They were also living very poorly. They needed bicycles, because many of them had more than one church.

I got to be very busy so fast. I also spent a few days at Kalighat, and that was horrible. I would sit on the side of a person's bed and hold them like a baby. Most of them weighed less than a hundred pounds. Some of them a lot less. They would take hours to die . We tried to feed some, but they would just bring it up again. Their beds were on a concrete pedestal, with a two inch thick vinyl washable mattress on top. The concrete was easier to wash with hoses. All of them were in pain. They would whimper and cry and eventually die. It was terrible. For them and for me.

If you were with me right now, I would pretend to make the noises that they made, and you would probably start to cry too. They didn't speak English, and even if they could, they were past speaking. I prayed for all of them, but I'm not sure that it had any effect.

Mark Buntain never ever came to the "Bengal Chambers" Hotel to visit me.

Mornings always began with the birds. People would go to bed with the sun going down and wake up when the sun returned. So did the birds. We had very large trees outside of the Bengal Chambers, and like everywhere in India, only bars on the windows. As soon as the sun began to rise, the crows began to talk. Thousands of them. The noise was incredible.

The Pastors I met wanted teaching. It simply wasn't available. Especially things about the Holy Spirit. They had been operating without the power. I was welcomed everywhere.

Every day, I was upset with all of these poor people living and dying on the sidewalks. One day I sat in a restaurant and some white people were also there. One man gestured for me to join them, and then they had many questions. What had I done back in Canada. What experience had I had, dealing with Government officials. They liked the fact that I had an audience with the King of Tonga. Eventually they told me, that they were all Medical Doctors, and they needed my help. This man, who was doing all the talking, was Jack, who I met many times after that. He liked to drink beer and he also had a girlfriend, who was a foreign correspondent for some British agency, and who was always taking notes. What these Doctors wanted was, for me to see the right Government person, to give these Doctors permission to do operations and generally take care of all of the people who were living and dying on the sidewalks. They wanted to set up large white tents on the parade square, beside the Howrah Bridge, which crosses the Hooghly River. It's like the George Washington Bridge. It's the bridge between Howrah and Calcutta and the Hooghly is the eastern tributary of the Ganges river.

They could finance the tents, and bring in Nurses from many countries, but they needed the government to supply security guards, like army soldiers, and most important, official permission to do all of this. They could supply about fifty foreign doctors. I started to make enquiries, and finally was told to meet with the Minister of Health. It took weeks. I saw so many underlings. They all wanted bribes to make an appointment.

The Howrah Bridge

Finally I got to see the Minister. What a grand office. And an outer secretary as well. We were served Chai and some treats, and then I made my request. He said he would see what he could do, and then, I was to come back next week.

The next week he said, "Mr. Peters, you really don't understand our situation, and our Hindu religion. First of all, the Communist Government here controls everything. Therefore, this would become a Federal issue, and for that, I would need to see the Prime Minister, Indira Gandhi, in

New Delhi. She was the leader of the "Indian National Congress Party". West Bengal had voted for the Communist party, instead of Indira's party.

Second, the Minister said, "we Hindu's believe that the Gods have determined that some people should be affluent, living in opulence. The Gods have also determined that some people should be poor, and live in abstract poverty on our sidewalks, and we really have no right to interfere with the decision of the gods.

I left very discouraged, by this totally callous, insensitive attitude. I reported this to Jack, and he suggested I go to New Delhi. In the meantime they decided to do operations in rich people's homes. Right on kitchen tables. Without proper anesthesia. Without proper blood transfusions. And many people died. And many were saved.

After many months, I met a Catholic priest named V. J. Pavamani. He liked my teaching, and we talked about everything. He also told me much information about Mother Theresa. One day he called on me and said that Mother Theresa wanted to meet me. I was glad to go. She was strange in every way. What the world didn't know, is that both her and Pope John Paul were very Pentecostal. Both spoke in tongues, and both had great Christian accomplishments. If you were to visit Mother Theresa, she would ask you a question, and the entire time you would sit across from her, she would be quietly speaking in tongues. Mark Buntain was the same.

Mother Theresa was full time in the company of the Lord, seeking instruction.

Ron in Calcutta wearing a Kurta

This day she asked me if I would help her with the problem in Calcutta, with drug addicts.

You see, all of Europe and Asia were sending their addicts to Calcutta, because of the price of drugs. An addict in Europe would need to do crime, to support the habit. In Calcutta, one or two dollars a day could support the habit. But they also died.

Cliff Richard donated half a million pounds, and some others had sent money, and Mother Theresa had some donations, and she bought a compound in Narendrapur. Sixty five acres, which had belonged to a very rich surgeon. This place had a mansion with a 9 foot wall all around the property, and a very large man-made lake, beautiful jackfruit trees, and a living room, that was like a basketball gym. Upstairs we had sixty beds side by side. There was a good kitchen, and a large garden.

All around the lake, near the house, were steps going down into the lake. About a hundred feet of steps curved as they went around the lake at the back of the house. At the entrance to the front yard, there was a 10 foot metal gate, and the house had huge double doors, with a metal gate in front of these doors, with big locks. A gang, led by a woman, bombed their way into the compound, and killed the whole family. The house came on the market, and it was perfect for a drug re-habilitation place. It had been operating for over a year, and now Mother Theresa wanted me to run the place.

VJ Pavamani drove me to the place and introduced me to everyone. They were all high, and the place was a total pig pen. The refrigerator had mold everywhere, there was no food, and nothing had been done for a very long time. VJ left, and I was now in charge. I got them all to stand in a straight line in the living room, and then I prayed. I raised my hands and arms and said, "Father God, heal all these men. Come Holy Spirit". They all fell down, onto the floor. It took a while and then slowly they all got up.

They were changed. They were healed. I asked them to all sit down on the benches around the room, and then I told them how Jesus had just healed them all, of drugs. Up until today, they had a system, of a little less drugs every day. The man dispensing the drugs, was also an addict. Consequently they got as much drugs as they wanted. Today was the last day of their addiction. I asked God what I should do now, and he said, "you will teach them". So I started a Bible school.

But first, we had to clean up the whole place.

We organized a huge laundry. The place really stunk. The kitchen needed a disinfecting. I assigned them all to different tasks, and they were good.

The bedding took two days. I had some men go with me, back to town, and we bought supplies. Bibles, writing paper, pens, toilet paper, food, cleaning supplies, etc.

We set up tables in the living room. I had 54 men to teach. It worked quite well.

We had a knife fight one day, and one man cut another. I fixed it.

The beds in India are about one foot high, and are two by twos, about two feet wide, and 5 foot 8 inches long. The frame has binder twine strung across the entire frame about every two inches. No mattresses, and because it's hot, we cover with a sheet for mosquitos. I'm six foot two, so the bed is a bit short.

There was a very large picture of Cliff Richard in the main hall.

One morning I woke up very early. The crows start talking when the sun rises, and it becomes very noisy. I looked up and saw a king cobra about a foot above my face, flicking it's forked tongue at me. I became extremely still, and in my head I was praying very hard. It seemed to take a very long time, but finally the snake went down and slithered out of the window. Our windows don't have glass, just metal bars. I called the men, and they took five foot sticks and went outside to find the cobra. In all the time we were there, we never saw it again. I had been teaching about water baptism, and within a couple of days, everyone wanted to be baptized. We had the perfect swimming pool lake, so one at a time, we went down the steps into the lake, and I baptized them in the Holy name of the Lord Jesus Christ. As I was about to baptize the third man, one of the fellows yelled, that there was a poisonous snake swimming right toward us. I turned around and it was now ten feet from us, about four feet long. I yelled at the snake, in the name of King Jesus stop, and be gone. Get thee hence Satan. I didn't know that snakes understood English, but that snake turned around, and swam toward the other shore, and we never saw that snake again. I continued the baptism. The guys were impressed. God has a way of confirming the word, with signs and wonders.

The village of Narendrapur was just outside of our gate. People could see us through the bars. When the men got saved, there was no trouble at all. But when we had the water baptism, all hell broke loose. Satan was furious. The entire town of Narendrapur came out and started throwing rocks over the wall. And pointed sticks. (I was glad, that they had no bows and arrows.) Then they started banging on our gate with metal bars, and then they got pots and pans and metal things and started banging. It was terribly loud. It went on all night, and during the night they threw firebombs over the wall. And sticks that were on fire. Our men quenched all the fires. But it was very dangerous.

I must confess to you readers, that my entire time in India, I was never afraid. I always knew, that if God wanted to kill me, he could have done it way back in Canada. He didn't send me on this long Mission, to die. The banging went on for three days. It was really horrible. We used pillows over our ears, and it was still noisy. I did much praying. We would all hold hands in a big circle, and I taught them also how to pray, in times of trouble. I told them, that you can trust God.

What I learned personally, was that Satan doesn't get upset when people get saved. But Satan gets furious when people get baptized. It's when we put on Christ, and receive him, that we get power against Satan.

(Galatians 3:27) He gets even more furious, when we get the baptism of the Holy Spirit. Bad things always happen. But God is there on our side. Greater is he that is in you, than he that is in the world. (1 John 4: 4)

We made it through this awful event, and nothing was damaged. Just a lot of junk in our yard.

Another day, I was reading my Bible early in the morning, as the men started to come downstairs. I sat on one of the benches, at the far end of the big hall. I was barefoot, in shorts and a t-shirt. It's hot, even in the morning. One of the men came toward me, and then in a whisper said "Sahib, don't move". I questioned. "Why". He said," there is a very bad snake under your bench."

Ok. How would you feel?

I'm bare foot with shorts, and a bad snake is behind my legs. I said, "what does he look like?" He said, he is this long and white. It was maybe 18 inches long.

I became paralyzed on this bench. After several minutes, all of the men stood about thirty feet from me and watched. I got fed up with all this, and I did my best basketball jump, straight up onto the bench. I almost lost my balance. It was close. What a relief. Then the men got sticks and the little snake evaded them for a bit, and then they killed it.

To go into Calcutta, I had to walk about a mile, through very dense jungle with grass, about seven feet high on both sides. The path was about two feet wide. Then I would take a ricksha taxi, (a man on a bicycle with a 3 foot wooden seat at the back) from Narendrapur to Garia.

The small bus in Garia had about ten seats and usually thirty people.

The motor is beside the bus driver, and it is supposed to be covered.

The drivers usually take the cover off, so they can quickly work on the motor if necessary. Consequently the fumes from the motor, comes right into the bus, and it is very nauseating. Garia is a city of almost two million, and the bus terminal is about an hour from Narendrapur. Then a two hour trip into Calcutta, with this small bus, packed on the inside, so the other peoples sweat comes into your clothing.

One day I was at Mother Theresa's office, and I was very busy. She came to me and said, "there is a girl here, working at Kalighat, and she is from Dublin, Ireland, and she wants to go shopping, and has no idea where to go. Please take her shopping." I said, "You know I have no time for this. I have things to buy, and then I need to get back." She said, "do it as a favour to me."

So I did. I had a wonderful time with this girl.

And then I took her back to Mother Theresa.

Isobel and I talked about my work, and I also asked her, what she knew about the Holy Spirit. She said, "I speak in tongues, and sometimes I prophesy". I said, "how is that even possible since you are Catholic. How did you learn this?" She said, "from my Priest". I asked, "how did he learn this?" She said, "from God. He prays a lot, and asked God what he should do about the Holy Spirit, and God baptized him with the Holy Spirit". I already knew this was possible. It was happening all over the world. Joel chapter 2: 28-29 was coming to pass. I had fallen in love with this girl named Isobel. She gave me her phone number, and address in Dublin, and I gave her my parents phone number. When I left the building, I prayed and asked the Lord, "can I marry this girl"?

And the Lord said, "no". I went back to Narendrapur.

Another time, I had been shopping in Calcutta, and when I got back to Narendrapur, I started to walk into the jungle path, and an elderly man, with beautiful long white hair, was walking behind me, and he said, "where are you from". I told him . We began a conversation, and he was very pleasant. But he had to walk behind me because the path was narrow. All of a sudden there was a long snake coming out of the grass ahead of me, and then it slithered straight down the path away from me. I followed at a safe distance, because I wanted to see if and where, it might go back into the tall grass. Then I looked behind me and the old man had stopped and was gesturing with his hand for me to come back to him. I went back, and he said, "What are you doing"? I said, "I wanted to see where the snake was going". He said, "Don't you know how dangerous this snake is. Even if you are on a horse, he can catch you. If he thinks you are bothering him, he will kill you." I was learning.

Another time, I was in Calcutta (now changed to Kolkata) and I was down town, when suddenly there was a Sandstorm. You could see it coming. People were running for shelter everywhere. I had no idea what to expect. Suddenly, it was over me, and it really hurt. Sand blasted by a storm, you cannot see anything at all, and the wind is incredible, and it's hard to stand, and you cannot see where you are going. All you have is a memory, of the last thing you saw. I still don't know how it happened, but a man pulled me into one of those lean-to homes against the wall of a building. Perhaps I had bumped into his home, and he realized someone was outside. This was a place about eight feet long and five feet wide. And this man and a child were in there, and a lady on a mat bed, who was really sick. Actually she was dying. She was starting to go unconscious. He was in terrible shape because he didn't know what to do. I couldn't communicate with him, but I gestured in sign language, that I wanted to pray for her. He nodded and I did. I laid hands on her head, and prayed a healing prayer, and she was healed. Right there in the middle of a sandstorm.

Wow. I suddenly realized that God had arranged the sandstorm, otherwise I would have never gone inside this poor home, and done God's business. I still don't know what her sickness or disease was, but anyone who would have seen her, before I prayed, would have confirmed, that she was actually dying. Both of them were overwhelmed and were crying. I said "Ishu Prabu Hai" which means "Jesus is Lord".

The storm ended after an hour, and I went back to Narendrapur.

In my bedroom, which was downstairs, there was a small room like a closet. It had a lock on the door, and I never gave it much thought. I really didn't need that closet, and I thought perhaps VJ, or Mother Theresa had used it for storage. Perhaps files or something. But then one day, I got curious, and also thought, if I use this closet, it can be like a vault for me if I buy a lock. So it was pretty easy to undo the metal, that was holding the lock, and suddenly I was in. There were cardboard boxes full of pictures. Pictures of little children. Most all of them looked like they were street people's kids.

Thousands of them. I realized that someone was running a "help the poor little children scam" and we'll send you a picture of who you are sponsoring. Some of the men heard the noise of me breaking the lock mechanism, and were standing there, like they had seen a ghost.

Later one of the men said to me, you are in very big danger now. You must leave Calcutta immediately.

He said it several times. Also one of the men had left the compound and had already gone to Calcutta. I prayed, and the Lord showed me to leave now. I did.

I packed some things and left quickly. After I got off of the bus in Calcutta, I thought I might go to Mother Theresa's before I go to the airport.

I never made it. Two men were shooting at me, but they were either very bad shots, or God was misdirecting their bullets. I ran and zigzagged and got away, and caught a bus, and then another bus, and finally got to the airport. I had my essentials in my shoulder bag. My money, my credit cards, my passport, my Bibles, my address book, and a couple of clothes things.

At the Airport, I quickly booked my trip to New Delhi, and there was a raised area, about six feet higher than the airport floor and I went up there, and sat down, and just like that, there they were. The two men that were shooting at me. I knew God would protect me. I didn't see any advantage in talking to security people. What proof did I have of anything. And why would they risk shooting me in the airport. All they really wanted, is for me to leave. The gang was caught if I didn't leave.

I left. I boarded the plane, and felt a real peace come over me.

CHAPTER 18
New Delhi

Amazing missionary adventures

Again, I knew the Lord had another plan for me, in New Delhi. I found a cheap Hotel near Narula's Hotel, on Connaught Circus, downtown. Narula's also had the best food in New Delhi.

New Delhi had 10 million people when I was there this first time.

Today it has over thirty two million people.

In 2022:
Delhi has 32,065,760
Mumbai has 20,961,472
Kolkata has 15,133,888
Bangalore has 13,193,035

New Delhi is a modern city now, but when I came there, it still had people living everywhere on sidewalks and in lean-to's against buildings. It was old and amazing. The shops all along every sidewalk were very interesting. The downtown core was a huge circle, called Connaught Circus. The British built their cities with a circle in the middle, and with the streets in spokes, going out from the circle. I remember one of the times I left the Bengal Chambers in Calcutta, just to go around the block, I got very lost, because there just isn't any such thing as going around the block. Four right turns doesn't bring you back home.

I took ricksha taxis everywhere. I was learning the city. I tried to see Indira Gandhi, to solve the Howrah Bridge parade square problem, for the Doctors. For three weeks they delayed me. Finally the Minister of Health saw me and said "if West Bengal votes for the Congress 1 party, then they would give immediate approval. But as long as the Communist party is in control, if they gave approval, it would look like the Communist party had done a very benevolent thing for the people of Calcutta. The Congress 1 party could not afford that.

I lost.

One day I went to Karol Bagh, where I met an older man named Rev. Roly Beecham, who had a good church. He liked my preaching and let me preach many times. He also knew many other preachers, and soon I was involved again. One day I met an American, Tim Kimbrel, and he knew of a place I could probably stay. It was a difficult place to find, but Sister Alice had rented this house, and there was also a young man from New Zealand there, named Lucas Giacometti. They also had a couple of servant people, and I rented a room. It wasn't close to anything that I was involved with, but it was good.

I soon learned what a saint Sister Alice was.

She had, over twenty years, started about 100 churches. Eventually, I visited many of them, and worked with them.

Alice had also worked Hong Kong, and taught school there, and also in Indonesia. Alice Shevkenek wrote a short book called "Oh Lord, Just one more soul". On page thirty she wrote" I love to introduce myself as a donkey for Jesus. It was a donkey that carried Jesus into Jerusalem, and this donkey has taken Jesus into many countries, cities, towns, and villages. And wherever I have taken Jesus, sinners repented, sick were healed, demons were cast out, and many were filled with the Holy Spirit. You see, that's what preaching the gospel is all about. We just bring Jesus to the people, and the Holy Spirit testifies of Him. He convicts them, draws them, cleanses, sanctifies, and justifies them when they repent.

Then He reconciles them to God, and has them legally adopted, into the family of God. What a wonderful salvation!

Sister Alice said I should contact Sister Nathaniel, in Safdarjung, at Laxmi bai Nagar, in the south of Delhi, past Ringi Road, near Camel Cinema. Sister Nathaniel offered me the rooftop room, which had been Sister Alice's home, for many years. It was great.

Sister Nathaniel owned three large schools and knew every pastor in Delhi. I got to be very busy preaching everywhere.

One of my favourites, was in Sunshine Colony, where I did nighttime meetings. Many got saved, and we did large baptisms.

I also worked with some churches in Karol Bagh.

Then I met Pastor K.V. Paul Pillai, who had a large church, and he also had written about ten good books. He was always very keen on the power of prayer, and the influence it has, on a person's ministry growth. I worked with his church for many weeks and loved it.

One day, he took me to a place out in the country, which housed blind people. We both went in and prayed with many, but since I could not communicate with them directly, due to their language, it wasn't very fruitful. I prayed for them to get healed, but nothing spectacular happened. I have since learned, that if serious healings are to take place, I need to remove all negative people out of the building.

Another time we drove far into Haryana State, and Paul took me to an orphanage, which had three stories. The place had a nine foot wall, two feet thick all around, about 50 acres of property. I should mention that about every fifteen feet, there were angle brick wall braces going out about ten feet. A huge metal gate and all of the buildings were raised about 8 feet higher than the land. This was because they bought the property cheap, and found out later, that it floods most years. The orphanage building had a floor for dormitory, a floor for school, and a floor for cooking and eating. This entire building was a square, with floors on all four sides, and in the middle down below, was a playground park.

When we went into the building, there were no children and only a few staff. It turned out that all the children had Malaria. When I went into the dormitories, they were in bed, freezing and crying. One by one, I laid hands on their heads and these children got healed. I prayed for everyone of them. And they all got healed. It happened to Jesus too. (St. Luke 4 :40).

Then I got to talk to them all and was that ever great. Telling them how great our God is.

There was a large church being built along the left side of a long driveway. At the end of that driveway was a bible school and a chapel. And over to the left was the dormitory, for all the Bible school students.

Way over to the left against the wall area, was a large man-made lake, which was actually a fish farm. They grew their own fish, (Machalai). They also had goats and sheep and cows.

Many of the Bible school students also had malaria. I prayed for them too.

(I had taken Quinine pills, before I went to India. Also before I went to Fiji.) I was asked to stay and teach, and I agreed. This was very unexpected, since I had other commitments back in new Delhi and Karol Bagh.

But I prayed and the Lord directed me.

The sleeping was difficult, with a short bed and a large mosquito net over me. And a thousand mosquitos trying to break through the net all night long. The food was different. Very spicy. Everybody had chores to do. Including me. Everyone helped. I washed bedding. And hung it all to dry. I taught the children. I taught the Bible school students. And it was very enjoyable for me. They were all keen.

So was I.

I was constantly amazed, how the Lord was opening doors for me, and giving me just the right people to work with. I was there for a very long time. I loved it.

Many of the graduate Bible school students went home to be pastors. When the Bible School season was over, I went back to New Delhi, and was sent by the Lord to churches outside of New Delhi.

My first long trip was north to Sirsa. I had no plans and knew no one. Just the Lord said, "go" and I took a bus. I was walking along the main street of Sirsa, and a Sikh man approached me, and asked me many questions in perfect English. He had been a high school teacher and Principal. He had also been in the army for a while. He invited me into his home down the road, for Chai. It was a grand home. We had Chai, and later this man insisted I stay with them overnight. I handed him four hundred Rupee's, and he pushed my hand away and said, "don't insult us. You are our guest. You will stay for our dinner." And I did . The next morning I told this man I had come here to hold meetings to teach, and he said he knew just the right place. He also said he knew everyone in Sirsa, and he would make all the arrangements for people to come. I couldn't believe it . With one man on the road, God had arranged everything. And he was not even a Christian. They came. Several hundred. Farmers mostly. All sitting on the floor of this building. Cross-legged. I never could sit like that. And I taught. I tried to make it interesting, and God gave me exactly the right words. We had salvations, and the next day we had baptisms. And I stayed with that gentleman the entire time.

From Sirsa, I went to Pehova. Many rectangle buildings with round roofs. All made of mud. And a door in the center, but no windows. At nighttime, all the blankets were placed on the floor, side by side, and in the daytime all the bedding was hung on the poles which were from side to side above our heads. We ate sitting on the floor. They cooked outside with a cow manure stove (they used cow manure as fuel, to burn on a little pot stove. They also used cow manure to cement the floor we slept on. They also had cow manure drying on all the concrete walls around the city. And I slept with a very nice family like this. I gathered people from around these houses and taught them, with an interpreter, that God miraculously gave me. Just one young man, who was educated. People got saved, and we baptized them. My interpreter was the first person I met in Pehova. He just happened to be keen on helping me.

When our Father God (the Great "I Am that I am") says he goes before us, I can testify to that.

That's the same great "I AM" that talked to Moses. (Exodus 3: 13-14)

In Deuteronomy 31:8
And the Lord, he it is that doth go before thee,
he will be with thee,
he will not fail thee,
neither forsake thee,
fear not, neither be dismayed.

This same God made me promises, before I ever started preaching, and not once has he let me down.

From Pehova, I went to Karnal, and met a man who went to a church there. He wasn't a strong Christian , but he knew the pastor. I baptized him a week later.

God opened the door for me again.

I really wanted to go into Punjab, to Ludhiana and to Jalandhar, but I could only go as far as Chandigarh.

The border customs men, said it was far too dangerous, and I should go back to Delhi as quickly as possible. They were killing tourists on buses etc.

It was all because the Hindu's from New Delhi had raided the Golden Temple. Nearly three hundred people were killed when the Indian Army, instructed by Indira Gandhi, stormed the Sikh Golden Temple at Amritsar, Punjab. Sikh's were retaliating by killing anyone from India.

A month later, I met a pastor in New Delhi, who was corresponding with Pastors in Punjab. He knew of my teaching and said the pastors in Punjab could come to New Delhi, if I would teach them. I made arrangements with the YWCA Hotel, who had a large meeting room, and rooms for the pastors to stay. We had about fifty pastors. I had a printing house print up sheets of my teachings, for the pastors to take back with them. I taught them for one week. Every morning, every afternoon, and every evening.

I didn't hand out the sheets until the last night. I had many letters later from those pastors, inviting me to Punjab when things would settle down.

I never did get to go.

I always wore the white Kurta pajama pathani suit.

I also wore a wooden cross on a chain which was 4 inches long. It all helped to identify who I was, anywhere I went.

Many times, I got to pray for people who recognized the cross. My cross does not have a Jesus on it. I was asked sometimes, why no Jesus on the cross, and I would respond, because he is risen. That cross hangs in my office now.

One night, I had been teaching a bible study near downtown, and then I took a taxi to Narula's, because I was hungry. By the time I finished eating, it was getting late, and the night was hot and lovely, so I decided to walk to my Hotel. It was a couple of miles across the railway tracks, to the Natraj Hotel.

As I was walking, all of a sudden a jeep, with four men, came behind me quickly, and stopped and four men got down and yelled at me, to give them my bag. I had a shoulder bag, which I had a shoemaker specially make for me, with a four inch wide strap around the top, so that it wouldn't hurt my shoulder, because I carried my Bible and much stuff. They wanted my bag, because every one knows that tourists have money and passports and valuables.

I put the bag on the ground, and took a martial arts stance, and with my hands, I gestured for them to come forward, and said, "OK, who wants to be first."

All of them, at the same time, ran as hard as they could, back to the jeep and squealed the tires, and drove away fast.

Then I realized it wasn't me. What they saw, was probably an angel behind me. I prayed and thanked God, for once again protecting me.

Psalms 91:10

For he shall give his angels charge over thee,

to keep thee in all thy ways.

Sister Nathaniel had a friend who was having a baby at Safdarjung Hospital. The baby had something wrong with it, and she asked me to go and pray.

Most American and Canadian people, consider India to be a bit backward, and third world, because of the way East Indian people dress. What they should know, is, that even back in the 1980's, medicine was more advanced in India, than in America. They were already using micro T.V. camera scopes, to do operations. They already had graduated eyeglasses, when we only had bi-focals. You could buy these graduated eyeglasses right on the street, on Connaught Circus. They also had better medicines.

Safdarjung Hospital was a training hospital, and many foreigners came there to study advanced medicines, and procedures.

However some things were still different. When I came to see the baby, there were ten people all around the bed, and mats, so that they could sleep there. When one person is accepted into the hospital, the whole family comes, and camps out around the bed, twenty four hours a day. I prayed for the baby, and it was healed. Then I prayed for a few more people in the hospital.

I was getting into a routine, and loving it, but after some months, the Lord told me to go to Bombay.

CHAPTER 19
Bombay (now Mumbai)

Amazing missionary adventures

Bombay had everything.

The worst slums.

The richest people.

The best restaurants.

Great hotels.

Trains that leave every five minutes.

People living on the sidewalks.

Rats everywhere.

Ships in the harbor that don't ever dock at the wharfs.

Bombay is a harbour city, by the ocean. In places, it is a very beautiful city.

What was interesting, is that the ships unloaded out in the harbor, not at the docks. The rats would contaminate the cargo. I met a ships captain, who had a cargo of grain, donated by the Canadian Government.

His ship was way out in the harbor, and he was waiting for the paperwork to sail to Dubai, with this grain as soon as it was sold and paid for.

He and I were at the Ambassador Hotel, having a nice, classy dinner, when below us, under the table, I saw a huge rat.

I signaled the waiter, and he insisted that he would take care of it imme-diately. Very soon, he was under the table with a large cage with bait inside, and the rat calmly walked in, as if he had done it many times, and the waiter carried the trap outside, let the rat go, and came back with the empty cage.

After telling this Captain what I did, he said his Dad and Mom went to an Anglican church all the time, but he found it very boring. He said he had a "prayer book" in his cabin, which he would use on occasion. I asked if he thought he was going to heaven. He said, probably not. I asked him if that concerned him. He said, not when I'm on shore. Only when I'm in rough seas.

I asked him if he knew that God actually controls the rough seas.

(Psalms 107: 21 -31) But he didn't want to pray with me.

I left saddened and then the Lord reminded me that sometimes you just sow seeds.

I found a room in a tall, very old building, near Nariman point, across from the ocean. It had an old elevator, with those metal expansion bars for a door, but it didn't work. So I had to walk up five floors, but the room was fine. Next morning, I grabbed my bag, and was off to find out, what God had for me today.

When I got to the front door, as soon as I opened the door, there were three Hindu priests in those diaper looking things, with lots of white and red paint on their faces and three wicker baskets with lids. As I opened the door, they lifted the lids and three black cobras were flicking their tongues at me, three feet from my face. I yelled out "Jesus" and they turned around and ran as hard as they could back to the main sidewalk and then ran east along the sidewalk, as fast as they could. They were all barefoot and around forty five years old. I ran fast and couldn't catch them. They finally got away.

I realized what God was showing me. While in Bombay, count on Jesus for everything. There is an enemy.

I went walking again, and eventually found a Catholic Church and got to talk to the priest who was very interested in what I had been doing. He said that Mother Theresa had a group of Nuns at Juhu, and I should visit them. I did. It was a long train ride. They welcomed me, and I asked them what they wanted in the way of teaching. They said, " we have a very sick sister nun, who needs healing. We need to learn how healings work". I said I would teach them, but first take me to the Nun and come and watch.

That did it. The nun got healed, and now they were my best promoters. They wanted me to meet the bishops.

I did. I got to preach at the English service, in one of the big Churches in Santa Cruz. I was very careful not to over speak my welcome. Then I got to meet some priests in Bandra. The nuns wanted weekly meetings with me. I got to preach again at Santa Cruz. Suddenly I was busy. In the daytime, those nuns were washing laundry and drying it on those big rocks along the ocean shore. Many very rich people, also lived along the beaches at Juhu.

My schedule was full. I really didn't need more teaching meetings. Then I was introduced to Pastor S. Joseph of "New Life Fellowship" at Mahim. He had a large Church, and I got to preach there many times. I also attended the morning pastor meetings. I did some afternoon meetings with the church, in other parts of the city. We also had a water baptism.

One morning a group of pastors came to my room on the fifth floor, where I was living. It was very early in the morning. They had been up all night, and wanted me to come with them, because they had a demon possessed lady, that they could not do anything with. They said it was quite close.

They said that they could not cast the demons out. As we were walking, they began to explain that this woman had great powers and was very dangerous.

It turned out to be a couple of miles.

We all went upstairs to the third floor

of this large warehouse. I asked them all to stay near the stairs, and to pray fervently.

I said, no matter what happens, do not come any further.

She was in the furthest corner, sitting on the floor by herself. She looked intently at me. This was a very big lady, about 45 years old. I said that "I have come to help you". In perfect English, she said "I don't need help".

She had a strange very low, raspy voice.

She said "I know who you are. You are from Vancouver in Canada. You have been doing miracles there. Then she spent fifteen minutes telling me about my life in Vancouver.

Things no one knew. I was totally amazed.

Then I asked her to tell me, "Who are you"?

She gave me a very foreign name.

I realized that I was talking to a demon.

I asked, "what was it like in heaven"?

She told me. Then I asked, "How come you didn't stay there"?

She said there was war in heaven, and we were thrown out. I asked her what that was like, falling out of heaven?

She explained in great detail, how horrible it was.

We talked for about an hour.

I found out that there were hundreds of demons in this woman. I prayed, and then cast these demons out, in the name of Jesus.

Nothing happened.

I did this several times. Nothing happened. I had been told that nothing can stand against the name of Jesus.

I had already cast demons out in other places.

This woman was laughing.

Then I walked away, and asked God "what do you want me to do ?"

God told me.

Meanwhile the pastors were looking at me, thinking I was having the same results they had. I went back and switched over to tongues only.

I received tongues the night I got saved.

Until that moment I was never sure if my tongues were actually real. I had been teaching how powerful tongues were, but I had never experienced anything like this.

The demons started screaming everywhere, in English.

Above my head.

Beside each shoulder.

Up near the ceiling.

All over the room.

They were crying.

They were begging.

They didn't want to leave her.

They knew they had to go back to the pit.

It was actually horrible.

The woman was contorting and flaying around.

She had no control. She was being hurt.

Hurt enough to scream in pain.

I just continued to speak in tongues.

I'm not sure how long it took.

Eventually they were all gone, and the woman fell limp. I wasn't sure if she was dead.

What startled me, was when a pastor yelled at me, asking if it was over.

Then the woman came to.

She was crying.

The pastors all came in.

We found out, that she could barely speak English.

She was speaking "Urdu".

India has about 20 major languages, and about 200 dialects.

I only spoke Hindi, poorly.

I asked the pastors to lead this woman through salvation and pray with her.

They did.

She was already crying.

Eventually they walked her to one of the churches.

I went home.

Two years later Isobel and I came to Bombay, and we met this lady at a church.

She was teaching the Bible, to a group of families, that gathered every week.

She was also a very good singer.

Eventually her and I did five Bible studies every week around the city. She would interpret.

She was very talented. She had also learned better English.

But her devotion to King Jesus was amazing.

A few weeks later, I was asked by some elders in Pastor Josephs Church to go to Thana, a city about 29 Kilometers from Bombay (18 Miles) to pray for a single girl, who had cancer. We went as a group, six of the church members, and we were greeted by the parents, at a very wealthy home.

The parents were very anxious about the prayer.

They allowed me to go into her room alone. I knelt beside the bed and began to pray. This girl (about 35 years old,) was now less than 70 pounds, and curled up in the fetal position, and in terrible pain, and whimpering and crying. It was awful to watch. I prayed and asked God, "what is your will?" God said, "they are idol worshippers, and If they break their idols before midnight, I will heal this girl."

It was now about 5:00 pm.

I had seen the recessed enclave, where the two statues of their gods were standing. I went out and asked the parents to sit down. Our group was also in the room. Then I declared what God had spoken.

Everyone was in shock. Our church group had not expected this. They had all hoped they would be able to show this Hindu family how wonderful and powerful the real God is, and the miracle would persuade them, to become Christians.

The next seven hours were horrible.

Our Christian group spent most of it, on their knees praying. And in between, they made concerted hourly pleadings with the parents, to just pick up their idols and throw them to the ground outside. We were on the second level, and they had a large balcony. The parents insisted they couldn't possibly offend the gods like that.

Meanwhile, the crying of their daughter was so pathetic, that all of us were crying with her. Her weak voice accentuated her pain, and hopelessness. It was much like those hopeless people in Kalighat in Calcutta, that we held, until they died. They could no longer hold down any food, or water, and their crying was totally heartbreaking. I've never worked in an ICU, in a hospital, but I imagine that it's much the same for those nurses. Pray for them too.

We made a strong plea to the parents just before midnight, and then, at exactly midnight (we had been watching the clock just like everyone does on New Years Eve) this poor soul in front of us died. Everyone was overwhelmed. We cried and left.

All the way home, they were asking me questions.

I simply answered that right from the beginning, God has stated that he is a jealous God. He will have no other Gods before him. (Exodus 20:3-5)

It was a great lesson to the church. They all spoke of this event for weeks.

I loved this city and would have stayed forever, except my parents were encouraging me to fly home for Christmas.

The first leg was to London, England.

I was on British Airways.

The plane was full of East Indian passengers.

We were on a new 747 plane.

When we reached 36,000 feet, a flight attendant came to me and said,

"Would you please follow me, and bring your overhead baggage, and things." I was hoping I wasn't in trouble.

She took me upstairs, to first class.

I was asked, what I wanted to drink. In the meantime someone brought me a hot towel and a leather bag of toiletries, including shaving gear. Then I was offered a variety of snacks. Then they asked me, "did I want red or white wine". Later someone asked me if I would like my bed made up. The seats fold flat into a narrow bed. Soon I was fast asleep in a bed.

When I woke up in London, England, the flight attendant said everyone had already disembarked, and I was the last one. They asked if I wanted to wash up first. I couldn't believe my good fortune.

CHAPTER 20
Kelowna, B.C. Canada

Amazing missionary adventures

My Parents, and some others, met me at the Vancouver Airport. It was so good to be home again.

I was going to go right back to India again, after Christmas.

I prayed about what God wanted me to do now.

God said I should have meetings in Hawaii, and meetings in Fiji, and then fly to Tonga again.

My mother had saved all the letters, that people had written. So many were from the USA and Canada.

I realized that I had a following. I wrote to everyone, that I was going to hold a teaching seminar in Honolulu, from the fifteenth to the twenty-fourth of January, in the conference room, of a large hotel we had booked. Then I wrote to my friends in Fiji and said I would be there from February the first, to February the twenty-eighth. Then I wrote to Tonga and said I would arrive March 1st.

A week later, we started to get bookings, and we were amazed, at how many were coming.

I held two bible studies before Christmas. It was mostly a review of my travels. Also loved being back in our home Church. I looked at all the married people in Church and started to think about a wife. I asked God if I could have a wife, to go to India with.

God said to phone Isobel. I said, "what should I say to her?" God said, "ask her to marry you". Wow!

I tried to phone the number she had given me in Calcutta. Apparently there was some kind of major storm, and all the lines were down. My brother said, "Send her a telegram."

I did. We still have that telegram.

Only four lines.

I love you.
Will you marry me.
Ron Peters
My parents phone number.

That was before Christmas. It wasn't until the day after Boxing day, that Isobel phoned. She was crying. Then she told me what had happened.

Around September the Lord woke her, and told her, that at Christmas, that missionary from Calcutta was going to ask her to marry. She was working as the administrator of an Architectural firm in Dublin, Ireland, and she told her boss and her co-workers, and her sister, and her parents and all of her friends, that at Christmas, she would be getting married. Then Christmas came and went, and she was so upset, that somehow, she had mis-understood God. And now, Isobel was very excited and said," Yes, I'll marry you. Are you coming to Ireland? My parents want to meet you."

I said I was very sorry, but I'm booked right through until March. She was very disappointed, but asked if she should come to Hawaii then, to marry me? I said yes but come to Canada now. She did. She arrived at the beginning of January and stayed with my parents.

We tried to get married with the pastor friends I had in Kelowna. Not one of them would marry us, because Isobel was from Dublin, which makes her Catholic, and I was protestant.

I went to Hawaii, ahead of my family, to make the detailed arrangements there. Isobel stayed with my Mom and Dad.

CHAPTER 21
Hawaii

Amazing missionary adventures

When everyone arrived in Hawaii, I decided to contact some of my preacher friends in Hawaii. I had the same trouble again. Isobel was Catholic. Then my Mom found a Hotel preacher, that did weddings in Hotel lobby's. We made all the arrangements. The city of Honolulu issued a Marriage Certificate.

The reception was at a very nice restaurant across the street.

Mom had ordered all of the cakes.

My favourite cake is chocolate, with chocolate icing.

That was our wedding cake. Actually, there were also about twenty other cakes. January the seventeenth, we had the Wedding after the morning teaching. It was perfect. Only one very unusual thing. Remember the whistling man, the night I got saved, who whistled like birds? He spent the entire night teaching me about the Holy Spirit, the night I got saved. Well somehow, God brought him to my wedding.

I didn't have a best man, so it became George Madrigal. Still in the white suit, and red tie, and red socks, and white shoes. I was thrilled, that God had done this. I have no idea how he found us. We only made these arrangements the day before. I've never seen George again, since our wedding day.

At the end of January, Isobel had to go back to Ireland, to close out her apartment, sell her car, quit her job, and train someone new, etc. She was going to come back (to Nadi, Fiji) at the end of February, and then we would fly to Tonga, to have a honeymoon.

The meetings at the Hotel in Hawaii were perfect. The people who came from USA, were inviting people they met, and every night we had salvation and healing meetings. That was the best part. The Pilot from San Diego, who had been blind, and came to the luncheon in Santa Ana in California, had also come to these 10 days of teaching with his wife, and they were a joy to everyone. My Mom and Dad got to hear me preach, and teach, and it changed them too. Many Hawaii Christians joined us too. One lady who had a TV ministry, had invited people to the meetings and people came.

Someone arranged for all of my meetings to be recorded on those small cassettes. They made hundreds, and even a year later my parents were still sending out those teaching tapes to people who needed them. Usually people were sending money with their requests. We did not charge for the tapes.

We had about twenty-five different tapes. No one can play them now. Times change.

CHAPTER 22
Fiji

Amazing missionary adventures

Fiji is 3159 miles southeast of Hawaii. (5057 KM's)

It's a 6 hours and 48 minutes flight.

It was great to be back in Fiji. But I was missing Isobel.

I met paster Joseph again, and he wanted me to do some teaching. I also met Pastor John Lesu. There is a river halfway between Nadi and Lautoka . Pastor Lesu had a church there but needed a building because his church was growing. They currently had a small wooden shack but had already laid the foundation for their new church. I prayed with him, and God told me to tell him, that he would provide a building. He let me preach several times.

Across the river from Pastor Lesu's church was a community hall. Pastor John suggested that I start some meetings there, and the people from the surrounding area would come. I made up 1000 flyers and rented the community hall. This area was a very old sugar cane farming town. The hall was hardly usable. The floor had shifted and wasn't level anywhere. But I thought we could seat about two hundred people.

I was living at a motel near the Nadi Airport. One morning I went to the restaurant of the motel, when I saw a familiar face. It was the man I had met in Amman, Jordan. He had communicated with my parents and had now brought his family to Nadi. I told him that tonight I am starting meetings, and we left early to set up. Pastor John Lesu was there also. John took this man back to his church, late afternoon and showed him the foundation of his new church. This man gave Pastor John the money to finish the church. We were expecting people to arrive before seven o'clock. I had my guitar and started playing and singing. Some children showed up, and soon we had lots of children but no adults.

I wondered what God was doing. Finally I started the meeting . I taught the children several songs just like I had in Tonga. Then I told them some stories. But I decided to act out the stories.

The first one was about David and Goliath. I acted out every part. There was David's army. The children had to be David's soldiers.

The Philistine's were on the other side of the valley. Both David and Goliath walked down to the bottom of the valley. Goliath being so heavy made big stomping sounds. Then they both stopped, and Goliath waved his huge sword. He looked very scary. David was a short shepherd boy. David knelt down and prayed for God to help him win. Then he stood up. David had a sling, and he went and picked up five smooth stones. Who wants to help David get some stones from the brook? Then David practiced with his sling. He waved the sling round and round. Swoosh, swoosh, swoosh, and suddenly he ran down the hill closer to Goliath the giant. Then David stopped and took aim and swoosh, swoosh, swoosh, swoosh, he let go of one side of the leather straps, and the stone flew in the air and hit Goliath right between his eye's and the stone sunk into his forehead. I played Goliath now and my hand went up to my eye's and I screamed in pain and went over backwards and fell down hard. I didn't hurt myself, but the kids all laughed.

Then I said Goliath is dead. David has killed him . The war is over. Israel had beat the Philistines. God had helped David. I wondered what had happened while I was telling the story. I looked up, and there were adults all around the back of the hall. I could also see adults on the outside.

I asked the children, " who wants to hear another story. They all raised their hands.

So I did Jonah and the Whale. Actually a big fish. It was fun for me and them. Jonah was to deliver a message to the city of Nineveh, that God was going to punish Nineveh. Who knows how to say Nineveh. Good. But Jonah didn't want to do it. So Jonah got onto a ship to get away from God. But you can't hide from God. God saw the ship and made a big storm. Let's all make a very loud wind sound.

Louder. Louder. And the ship was going up and down. I got the kids to go up and down with their knees.

They held there hands out in from of them like I did.

Then the people on the ship realized it was all Jonah's fault and what did they do. They were afraid that the ship would sink. So they took Jonah and threw him off of the ship.

Who can help me throw Jonah off of the ship? We all did a two arm throw and threw Jonah over the railing of the ship. Now Jonah went into the ocean. But God sent a big fish like a whale. Hold your hands like this. Really wide, now close your arms around Jonah as he goes into the fishes mouth. Now Jonah is inside the fish. And there are weeds and fish food inside. OK everyone wiggle like you are inside the fish. And it stinks and it dark and it's horrible. Ok show me how you are inside of the fish. They all put their arms around their head and made bad faces. OK. How is Jonah going to get out of this big fish?

Jonah remembered God. Jonah yelled out "Thank you God, you can save me God." Then I had the children yell, "Thank you God. You can save me God."

What did God do?

He made the fish swim to shore and spit Jonah out onto the shore. Ok, all of you swim to shore and push Jonah out of your mouth onto the shore. They all did some pretty freaky moves and Jonah was on the shore.

Does anyone know what God wants us to do when we need help? Just like Jonah we say " Thankyou God, help us God. Save us God". I got them to repeat what I said, and they all said:

"Thankyou God, we know you can save us .

We know you can help us."

Who would like God to be your saviour?

They all raised their hands.

I did a children's version of a sinners prayer.

Then I turned to the adults and said, "are there any adults here who would like to repeat the sinners prayer with me?"

Several raised their hands. It Worked. They did it.

I then asked pastor John to say some words in Fijian.

He did.

In Samabula, I met a Pastor who let me preach several times. Until one night, I preached something different than what the pastor taught. That ended that.

Then I met a group of pastors from Nadi, who had a good church membership, but only poles and a tin roof for a church. But they were glad to have me there, and I loved working with this group.

Also worked with a church called Calvary Assemblies of God, in Lautoka.

Also preached with a church at 8 miles. They could really sing, and they also had those car springs, which they played like tambourines.

Isobel was coming back, so I took a bus to Nadi to meet her at the airport. I was really glad to see her again.

Then we went to Nausori to fly to Tonga.

CHAPTER 23
Tonga
(The second time)

Amazing missionary adventures

Tonga is 500 miles Southwest of Fiji. (640 KM's)

The flight is 1 hour and 45 minutes long.

March 3,1982 we were on the runway, ready to take off and then we just sat there. The pilot came on the intercom several times, saying that we should be taking off shortly. Finally, after over an hour, he said we were returning to the terminal. Then, when we docked, the pilot said we were being sent to a hotel, and they would send a bus to pick us up in the morning and try again. He said they could not get landing instructions in Tonga, due to a major storm.

The bus came for us the next day and finally, Isobel and I got to fly to Tonga.

They called it Hurricane Isaak. The storm in Tonga destroyed pretty much everything. We landed and went through customs, and then a group met us. All of us hugged and knelt and prayed. Everyone knew of the prophecy for the King, two years earlier.

The storm had torn up everything. Even the sea wall around Nuku Alofa was torn up. Many people had hid in church basements. The winds had torn off the corrugated tin roofs and the louvered glass windows and with everything flying through the air at over hundred miles an hour, it was amazing that not one person was hurt during the storm. The winds also blew out to sea, all of the straw homes around the island.

And all of the things they had in their homes.

After the storm eleven people were treated for minor things, such as glass cuts, stepping on nails etc.

A few days later we heard that two fishermen had drowned at sea.

Hurricane Isaak did this to hundreds of homes

A few homes had only roof damage because their walls and roofs were fastened to firm concrete foundations.

They said it was the most severe storm experienced in southern Tonga, in more than one hundred years. The people lost everything. They had no food, no clothing, no shelter , no cooking utensils, nothing. And it was still raining.

Relief agencies and the armed forces of Australia,

New Zealand, and other countries worked quickly to bring food supplies, latrines, water, medicine, cooking utensils, and canned goods. The army brought 1000 tents and tarpaulins and were helping to set them up. The Tongan people had never seen a tent before. They had never seen latrines before either. Nor did they like the canned food, but they were hungry.

Princess Maleniti and the Kings brother, who is the Prime Minister, and the red shirt is the head of the Peacekeepers in Tonga.

The churches in New Zealand sent hundreds of boxes of clothing (huge cardboard boxes).

Isobel knew how to sew and tailor, and she helped organize the women to re-sow the clothing. Tongan women were not built like new Zealand women, so all the clothing had to be re sown. And then dyed black . The boxes had modern clothes such as Hot Pants and peddle pushers, and sleeveless blouses. Everything had to be resown. They also made children's clothing and men's clothing.

The Prime Ministers (& Princess Malanites') house became the factory, for the next three months, to resew and dye black the clothing, sent from churches in New Zealand.

Hurricane Isaak was declared by the Tongan Authorities to have been the worst disaster in Tongan history, in part, because of the magnitude of the destruction of housing, public buildings, and livestock (95% of livestock were killed in some places.)

God said he would remove the blessing in Tonga if the King did not move his people back to righteousness.

From the time we arrived in Tonga, people were coming to me for prayer. People were repenting. When we started distributing food and water and clothing, in every village people would gather and kneel on the ground and lift their hands up and weep in repentance. Princess Malanite had a large Jeep, and we traveled to many villages every day, and the people knew what God had done.

The princess's Jeep was used for clothing delivery. Isobel and I had no time for each other, for about three months. We were so busy. This was going to be our honeymoon. But we had our commitments here.

Then the world health organization started to hold meetings about aid distribution. I was invited to attend those meetings, and Isobel typed up the minutes of those meetings.

It was very tense and stressful. I tried unsuccessfully to plead a case for the ordinary people. However all funding had to be sent to the Tongan government officials. (the Nobles)

Tonga was changed now. They repented and we knew God would return the blessing.

Isobel and the Princess delivering clothing parcels

The Tongan people are so kind. They had learned from my teaching, that it was dangerous to complain. Their humility was awesome. Now they were weeping and praising God for sparing them. Every place I went to, the people were repenting.

If I won the lottery, I would sponsor Havili and his group to tour America and Europe and Australia and New Zealand, for the purpose of revival.

Please go to "You Tube" and search: Take our Nation God again, by Havili Sefesi at Tapaita ILafehi Liava'as Funeral 07/01/16.

He was also the music leader at a small Tongan church.

Today he is the pastor of a large church, and he is an incredibly anointed singer.

Havili still plays the Guitar and sings. God gave me a first class helper for the two periods I spent in Tonga.

We still communicate.

Every nation in the world needs to have this attitude towards God. The attitude of repentance. I wish that every pastor everywhere, would play this video for his congregation, with the purpose of revival.

CHAPTER 24
New Zealand

Amazing missionary adventures

A few weeks later we flew to Auckland, New Zealand.

I had been there before, and it was good to meet old friends again.

I was invited to do a Full Gospel Dinner. I did not realize that God was still making all of our plans. Two Directors of the "Full Gospel Businessmen's Fellowship" were there.

They decided that night, to send Isobel and I, to fifteen cities, to do the same thing there. They also arranged a radio program for me. We were in a different city almost every week.

About once a week we would have two or three days in the same city, and I got to work with some churches. For me it was thrilling. For Isobel it was exhausting.

When we finished, we were invited to attend the Full Gospel Conference in Wellington, New Zealand . It was great and we enjoyed it.

Then a Pastor invited us to Nelson, NZ. And we stayed with his family for about ten days. They had a small house, and they gave up their master bedroom, and they slept on sofas in the living room. People were so kind.

The pastor and his wife in Nelson, NZ

We walked their beach almost every day.

We had meetings at the Church almost every day and we really enjoyed their hospitality.

On Saturday we had a Baptism in the Nelson river. About 20 people got baptized.

What was interesting, was that there were icebergs the size of large cars, floating down this river. I was in the water with the pastor for at least an hour, and neither of us caught a cold, or had our lower body frozen.

I remember that a few came up speaking in tongues.

I thought that was unusual, at the time.

In Christ Church, we got to stay with a family that had a Printing Business and also did book Binding. My red Bible was falling apart and needed an entire new cover. That man gave me my Bible, still red, that looked brand new, and I still use it today.

Christchurch is an exceptional city. And the people gave us a very warm welcome. We were busy every day for about a month. The churches were wonderful, and we had great results.

Eventually we flew to Sydney, Australia.

CHAPTER 25
Sydney Australia

Amazing Missionary adventures

Sydney resembles Vancouver, B.C., Canada.

But the people are very different from New Zealand people, or Canadians. I did get invited to two churches, but not to preach. However I met an Architect who invited me to do a Full Gospel Businessmen's dinner Banquet in Sydney.

We also met a couple from Armidale, who invited Isobel and I to stay at their house for a week.

Isobel on the sheep farm at Armidale

We took the train from Sydney, north to Armidale. The train went through a mountain range and that train was exceptionally cold. The heating system had broken.

They lived on a large sheep farm, and it was a great experience. They also had lots of amazing high ant hills . And lots of kangaroos. We also watched how they shave the wool off the sheep.

The Professor's house was marvelous.

He was an English professor at the University there. He introduced us to a Full Gospel Chapter Luncheon and then I did another banquet.

At the banquet, an Anglican Pastor who was there, invited me to speak twice at his church.

We did a bible study at a hall, and then went to the Anglican Church where we had a two great meetings

We eventually flew back to Sydney and began to make plans to fly to India. We did some meetings, and then we met a man at a meeting, who invited us to stay with him. He had a huge expensive house, and a Jaguar, and he let us stay at his house for a few days. He was former MI6 and had quite a past. He was a Christian, who invited us, so that he could learn more. Every window in his house had electric metal, bullet proof shutters, that he could operate remotely. He had awesome alarm systems, and escape things. And a vault room. He was British, living in Sydney, and had an amazing testimony.

One day he took us for a long drive into the country, and we stopped at a unique roadside restaurant, which had a hundred cars in the parking lot. We chose our own steaks from a huge refrigerator with doors opening to the patrons, and then we cooked our own potatoes, onions, steaks, and poured our own beer. It was fantastic. Everyone ate at picnic tables outside.

We also toured Sydney.

From Sydney we flew directly to Bombay.

CHAPTER 26
Bombay, India

Amazing missionary adventures

It was great to be back in Bombay. Nothing had changed. We found a cheap hotel called the Elphinstone. It wasn't far from the India Gate, where the Taj Mahal Hotel is. So we ate many meals in the Shamianna room, where the western food is really good.

The Elphinstone Hotel, Bombay, India

Isobel wanted to meet the nuns I had talked about at Juhu Beach, at St. Joseph's Church, where I had been teaching.

This is our first letter from Bombay.

If you could have been with me at the prayer meeting last Tuesday and heard Wilson crying before King Jesus, all of you would have cried with him. He came to the meeting an alcoholic. Sister Jesse, a nun, and a social worker has worked with him for more than two years. I prayed over him, and he was instantly delivered from both cigarettes and alcohol.

Wilson prayed like this, " God, Ron says to talk to you in the name of Jesus. I have been sinning again and feeling sorry for myself. I'm sorry. Please forgive me. Ron says that you still want to be my friend. I'm not worthy to be your friend, but I'll try. Thankyou for healing me tonight. Thankyou for still being my friend, Amen."

About fifteen people prayed, and they were all crying. They were apologizing to God for being name Christians, and they were asking God to let them be his servants, presenting their bodies a living sacrifice to him, servants of obedience unto righteousness.

Many people were healed later, and God was there.

God has opened the doors for me to teach again, and the people are anxious to learn.

Two Sundays ago, I preached In Bovrilla, at the

"Good News Center". I had preached on "How to hear the voice of King Jesus", and one girl about twenty two, got saved, and one boy about twenty also got saved.

It is always great to lead people to Jesus . We had lunch with some people out there, and then prayed for some more people. Late in the afternoon we took the long train ride back. The train was crowded, and it was difficult. It was also raining. When we finally reached Church Gate Station, Isobel and I and ten thousand other people headed towards the exits. At the first exit we tried , we were greeted with some Cobra snakes. We retreated and at the next exit there were more snakes. We tried five exits and there were snakes everywhere. We asked a policeman to help us, and he did. You see, these snake people think tourists will give much money to them, so they rush at you with these snakes. We got outside at the front entrance, and it was raining. Heading towards the underpass, we were confronted with more snakes. We ran towards the opposite direction, and there were more snakes again. There is an overpass for pedestrians, and we decided to escape by crossing the street this way. Halfway up the steps, all of a sudden there was another big Cobra facing us. Well, Isobel and I just about had heart attacks. We ran back down, jumped a wall, flagged a taxi on the road and made it back to our room. The next day, we found out that it had been a special snake holiday called "Nag Panch Me". People are supposed to buy milk for the snakes and the snakes are then so thankful, that they bless the people. Of course that's a lie of Satan. Anyway, we've made a note of the date for next year.

I was back at Kalina this Tuesday, and I know that the Lord wants me to do a lot of work with the Catholics again this year. Last Wednesday, a boy got saved at the Juhu meeting, and we had some very amazing healings too.

Also last Wednesday, I was getting off a bus with Pastor James and he made it off, but I didn't.

A young man blocked me with his arm, by holding on to the railing in front of me. I was coming down the stairs from this double decker bus. I was actually a bit angry inside myself, thinking how I'd like to Judo Chop his arm out of the way. And at the same time, I was reminded, how I must show Christian love, so I was very polite. In the meantime people were also pushing behind me, and I was not getting through to this young man, who was looking away. Finally, I spoke louder, and he looked and finally moved his arm. I jumped off, as the bus was leaving.

It was then that I realized that this had all been staged. They were a team. My bag had been neatly sliced wide open by a razor knife. About a twelve inch cut, in the center compartment. Just that morning, I had taken my camera out, to check something and I actually had forgotten to put it back into that compartment. All that was in there, was my raincoat. It got a few minor cuts. But what is truly amazing, is that there is another pouch pocket, in the same compartment, where we keep our passports, credit card, and all of our big money, and our airline tickets. But the thief got nothing. God answered our prayers and protected me. He also protected me from catching them in action, because I'd have probably been sliced by that razor knife. Isn't God great, how he protects his children. It cost me three rupees to get my bag stitched. God has great promises.

Psalms 91:10-11
There shall no evil befall thee, neither shall any plague come nigh thy dwelling. For he shall give his angels charge over thee, to keep thee in all thy ways.

While I was fasting for three days, God showed me some more truths in the Greek Bible.

In James 5:16 in Greek it says, "Confess ye therefore to one another your sins". I've been teaching to confess your faults one to another, but not your sins. Again I was wrong.

In doing this, it also becomes a fast track for a healing to take place.

This also ties in with:

Jeremiah 5:25
Your iniquities have turned away these things, and your sins have with-holden good things from you.

Tonight, as I was coming back into our building, after our leadership class at church, our "Chowkidar". that is, our watchman, was eating his supper. It was the first time in five weeks that I've seen him eating. It wasn't much, just rice and dahl, and roti which he told me cost eight rupee. I stayed and talked to him for a while about Jesus.

He tried to tell me that the Hindu God, the Moslem God and the Christian God were all the same God. So I told him no.

The Christian God is the only God. When you think about it, it is a bit strange to explain our God. That he is the only one, but that you can only come to him through his son, Jesus.

While we were talking, at least six rats ran around our feet. One rat ran right between his bare feet. He sleeps on the floor downstairs in the hallway, where we were talking. He gets three hundred rupee per month, and he is actually working twenty four hours a day. He gets short sleeps at night, because the Arab people are so noisy all night and often come home at three or four o'clock in the morning. And during the day, he also washes floors, changes beds and many other jobs. He doesn't get paid enough to eat more than one meal a day. He has a wife in Puna, a city six hours away. He tries to send her money. He has some helpers, about five of them. The others only receive one hundred and fifty rupee per month. And every day when we come out of this building, there are a hundred beggars outside, who don't have any income. I often cry and thank God that I have food every time I am hungry, and a good bed to sleep on. At night when we travel, the streets are all full of people sleeping on the sidewalks. Just laying down on the filthy sidewalks, and rats running around curiously and grabbing at garbage. Thousands and thousands of people sleeping in the open because they have no where else to go. And they are condemned people. Condemned to go to the lake of fire and brimstone, which is the second death.

Some people take offence to the fact that I call people who are not saved - condemned people.

St. John 3: 17-18
For God sent not his Son into the world
to condemn the world,
but that the world through him might be saved.
He that believeth on him is not condemned:
but he that believeth not
is condemned already,
because he hath not believed in the name
of the only begotten Son of God.

On Sunday afternoon as I was walking, I saw a man on the road and his leg was covered in blood. When I came closer, I saw that his entire knee area had no skin at all. And it was covered in flies. Flies were all down his leg too, attracted to the blood. It looked to me, like this had been done on purpose. The devil makes people do such horrible things. It helps them to be very good beggars. People who control these professional beggars, make a lot of money. You see people in train stations, who have eyes missing because of acid, and their face is raw flesh, and it really looks horrid. Then there are people who zip around on homemade skateboards, at traffic lights, begging to the affluent in cars. These people on skateboards often have no legs at all. Sometimes with all the strength of their arms, they will raise themselves to the windows, by hanging on to the door handles, and people feel sorry for them . And every where in the city, at every corner, women with babies beg, to the people in cars. And the children too. Running all over the streets, darting around the moving cars. It's absolutely amazing how these people don't get hit by the traffic.

In Calcutta, because of the millions of homeless who had no money for food, families dedicated one child to begging, by maiming them. Sometimes they cut off an arm. Sometimes they keep the child in a small cardboard box, until it is about three years old, and by then the legs are totally maimed, and useless. They place these children on a small piece of cardboard on a sidewalk, to sit in the sun all day, and they cry, and are going blind, and they are so skinny, and it is horrible to look at.

It's hard to believe that it can rain so much too. The humidity is so high, that it is close to breathing water. What is also amazing, is that almost every day, I am so busy, that I honestly don't even think about it. I just keep praising King Jesus that he promised me that "Nothing shall by any means hurt me". (St. Luke 10:19)

God is changing my course again slightly and opening more doors for me. On Sunday I preached at a huge slum called "Dharavi". This slum has about forty Lakh people and a lakh is 100,000. There were about 200 people at this meeting, and you would have enjoyed their sincere humble attitude of worship, and their extremely excited spirit filled singing, all in Tamil of course. But I spoke through an interpreter from Borivali, named Raviraj. In the end, we baptized three men, and three women. There was one woman who gave testimony of how she had been a Christian for many years, and for seventeen years, her life had been really awful. Her husband had remained a Hindu. And for seventeen years, she had been praying for him. And now, one of the three men we were baptizing, was her husband. Hallelujah !

God does answer prayer. Then on Sunday night, I was at another church. The pastor of this church gave the most hateful and angry Independence Day message. But he did not once quote a Bible verse, nor had he taken a Bible to the pulpit with him. It's a sign of the times. I read in a Time magazine last week how some Lutherans and Baptists don't endorse prayer in U.S.A. schools. I recall well, how we always recited the Lord's Prayer, to open the school day. Don't be surprised at what is happening everywhere. They all spoke about it. The prophets wrote about it, and we know, we are in the last days. We are well into the last days. Isaiah's Dad (2 Chronicles 26:22) told us about it in Amos 8:11-12.

But there is still time for us, and the great Prophet, Jeremiah is still encouraging you and I in Jeremiah 3:12-15.

Every Tuesday morning, I will be privileged to speak to 1900 students at the "Bombay Scottish School". Most of the students have Hindu parents, and they are the elite of the city. We had our first meeting this Tuesday, and God really helped me. I still have my Tuesday night class, with the Catholics at Kalina, in Santa Cruz east, and I have taught there six times now. We are hoping to expand this class from this house meeting to a Catholic school nearby, where many from that school will join us. I have a meeting scheduled with Father Victor Alphonso tomorrow and God willing, we will complete this arrangement. Following several days of prayer, God has shown me to have several classes with the Catholics in this city. So I am excited about that.

The Lord has also opened the door for me, with the Methodists, and I've got a second meeting scheduled with their leaders this week.

Johnny and Meeta of the Bombay Scottish School.

After a meeting at the Bombay Scottish School yesterday, I had the opportunity to go to the home of an elderly Christian lady, who apparently had been dying of cancer. When I got to this beautiful apartment home, the daughter who is married, ushered me into the living room, and told me that mama was in a terrible mood, and didn't want to be prayed over today. The Lord Immediately reminded me "that the steps of good man are ordered by the Lord, and he delights in his way." (Psalms 37: 23)

So I knew the Lord wanted me here, and that he would show me why my direction here, seemed to have this curve. We talked for a while, the servant brought Chai (tea), and this daughter was very excited about the little miracle God did for her on Sunday. She's a Catholic, and Sunday she got Baptized at New Life Fellowship. She was afraid, and not at all certain that she was really doing the right thing, but she did understand that it was an act of obedience to God. She had asked God to give her sign. And it was a miserable cloudy day, and several persons were baptized before her. They baptize most Sunday mornings at 9:00 am. Well, God did a miracle. As she was standing in the water with the pastor, the sun shone very brightly on her, and when they came out of the water, the sun was gone again and afterwards it rained. But for that brief moment, God shone on her, and she really knew it was God. God also spoke to me, as I listened, and I suddenly realized why God had delayed my praying for the mother. God wanted to give the gift of healing to this daughter. So I asked her if she had ever thought about being able to lay hands on the sick people, pray for them, and then see them get healed. She said "Oh yes, but she was never a good enough person to do that. So I told her that she was only good enough, because of the goodness of Jesus. Then I prayed with her, and asked God to give her the Holy Spirit, and then anoint her hands with the gift of healing. When we finished, in the perfect timing of Jesus, a lady in a white uniform came into the room and smiled and stated that mother wished to be prayed for now. Was this daughter ever pleased and thrilled. But she didn't realize that it would be her doing the healing prayer. She said "I don't know what to say".

So I said, "Just put one hand on your Mama's head and one on her stomach where the pain is, and repeat the words that I tell you. So we said, "In the name of Jesus, I bind you sickness. In the name of Jesus, sickness come out. Mama, be healed in the name of Jesus. By the stripes of Jesus you are healed Mama.

Rise up and walk Mama.

The pain left immediately.

Mama was poking fingers into her stomach, to see if there was any pain left. I walked out of the room and a moment later Mama was walking to a washroom. God showed the daughter, that she had actually received the gift of healing. Then, as I was leaving, I met her brother, who just happened to come there, at that precise moment. He ran after me to the elevator and asked me to pray for him privately. A Muslim, suffering from asthma, and when I prayed for him, he was instantly healed. He took some very big breaths, and now he was crying hard. We prayed together. His sister has prayed a long time for her family. Now they are getting saved, the others will get saved now too.

I've also had one meeting with Rev. Ed Lewellen of the Alliance Churches. Ed and Ruth are Superintendents of the six churches, that they have started around Bombay, and they have been here about twenty five years. Each church has about thirty people, except their latest one apparently has almost one hundred.

I get to pray for so many people. They come to our Hotel room or to the church, or I go to so many homes and God never lets me down. I'm excited that soon we will meet him in the air, and we will see him.

We started a weekly Bible study and prayer group in a home in Kalina, where we meet Tuesdays. Everyone gets a chance to express there needs for prayer. Avis, the Lady of this house, was so upset about her husband, who had been living with another woman for some time. She also has two children. So I prayed for her and told her to prepare herself to receive him back. At the next meeting she was still very sad, but she said a friend told her that on Tuesday night her husband had had much trouble with his girl friend. I saw her again on Sunday at church, and she said again, that a friend had told her that on Tuesday, her husband had another fight with his girlfriend. Always on a Tuesday. But she said there still doesn't seem to be any change, or any hope. I told her "nonsense".

Don't ever believe what you see in the physical. We don't walk by sight. We walk by faith. (2 Corinthians 5:7-8). If we pray to the true God, then expect results. I told Avis to hold hands with the children several times a day, and just thank God over and over again, for bringing Daddy home. Even though he is not home yet. Get it into your hearts.

Avis sent her friend to talk to her husband and he told this friend, to stay away, that everything with the girlfriend was fine, and not to bother him ever again.

Next Tuesday we prayed again, and I told Avis, "God is doing it. He will bring your husband home".

Just start to believe it and thank King Jesus for bringing him home.

On Saturday there was a knock on our door, and Isobel answered the door. It was Avis's servant man, and he said to come quickly with him. Isobel and I were not sure what to expect, and when we knocked on Avis's door, Johnny, the husband came out, and we all were in shock. He said he had become so miserable with his girlfriend, and all he wanted to do, was to come home to his wife and children.

We have met Johnny twice now, and he's home to stay. He has been to two of my meetings now, and he's so changed. He's on fire for God now. And you should see the kids. Are they ever happy. When I came the first time after daddy came home, Candy and Patrick came running to me, all excited and said "he did it, he did it. Jesus brought daddy home"

It's never by power, or by might, but by his Holy spirit. And the battle is not ours, it's his. We can move mountains, if we don't doubt in our hearts, and believe those things which we say. (St. Mark 11: 22-24)

One Tuesday night at Avis's home, there was a young boy about twelve years old, who needed prayer for an operation he was to have the next morning. Apparently the doctors had found a tumor on his brain the size of an egg and hoped to remove it tomorrow.

They were all hoping that the cancer had not spread.

We all prayed for him. The following Tuesday we saw the boy again, and he testified that the doctors had told him that the tumor just rolled out as if someone had already cut it out. He was fine now.

Last Sunday, Pastor Challow Daray of the Dharavi Church asked if I would teach the "Applied Word Center course" to the Dharavi Church, and also to the Bhandup Church. (this is a course that I have been writing for over a year and have recently been showing to a few pastors.) Because I am so busy again, we are going to try to combine one night a week with them. It's about a 90 minute travel time between the two churches when the buses aren't too full. We might resort to two meetings. And I've been invited to start a class at Borovilli, which is at the end of the train line. Last Sunday night, the Pastor of the Presbyterian Church in Colaba, asked me to preach at his Church, so we arranged meetings for the next three Sunday nights. They have first and second readings in their Church, so I had to Give Rev. Michael Sundar the Scripture references for the next three Sundays. I'll be speaking on "why prayers don't get answered, then "Prayer Power" and finally on " How to hear the Voice of Jesus"

This coming Sunday, I've been asked to speak at the Chapel, of the Bombay Scottish School at Mahim.

This past week, Isobel and I have moved to a one bedroom apartment at Vakola Bridge, in Santa Cruz. It will be much cheaper for us, and we'll have more room. We are very blessed to have an apartment.

The local people cannot rent apartments, even if they had the money, because of Indian law. A tenant can never be evicted, so people are afraid to rent to anyone. Therefore the rich buy apartments, and give them to their children as doweries, when they get married. In India, about 3 percent of the people are rich and ninety seven percent are poor. Of the ninety seven percent, half are below the poverty line, which means they don't have enough to eat. Often I say to Isobel, I wish the saints back home could see this street we are walking on. Little children huddled together in the rain, on the side of the street, sitting in the muddy filth, all sticking their little hands into the same bowl of rice, eating what little food someone has given them.

Yesterday, we saw one of the worst sights a human being can experience . A small girl, possibly six to ten years old, had been run over by a bus, and we always stop at accidents to pray for the victims. But they carried this one away in two parts, first the top half and then the bottom half. It was horrible.

The Gideons of Bombay have invited me to be their guest speaker from ten in the morning, to five in the afternoon at a teaching retreat, in Anderea, on October second. Praise God. I feel very honored, and I request your prayers on that day. Thankyou.

Our second letter from Bombay.

Isobel and I are thrilled with the way God is constantly opening doors for us to minister .

We are always so busy.

Our schedule is constantly gathering momentum here in Bombay, and we give all the glory to our King Jesus.

We currently have four Bible studies during the week,

One at Kalina,

One at Vakola, at our apartment.

One at Mahim

and one at Bandra.

Then we have our leadership class on Saturday night at Byculla, a Pastors meeting every Wednesday, Hindi lessons every Tuesday and Thursday, and preaching Sunday morning and Sunday night.

In between I get called to pray at various homes for the sick and other problems, several times each week, and often get taken to hospitals. We have almost no time to ourselves. And King Jesus is coming soon.

We'll be going to a village of (we think) about sixty thousand people, on the 27th of October, and we'll have salvation meetings there for four days. The place is called Manmad, and it's a seven hour train journey out of Bombay. We are also invited to an interdenominational conference from the 13th to the 16th of October at Mugti, which is about thirty-five miles from Pune. I'm looking forward to this conference, and we believe God will move mightily.

We have also been invited last Sunday, to come to Pune at the beginning of November for about ten days, to have salvation meetings there.

Pune (pronounced Poona) is about a 6 hour train ride south of Bombay. Manmad is east of Bombay. And October 2nd we have a meeting from 9:00 am to 5:00 pm with the Gideons, at Anderea. They have sent a lovely letter to me, confirming that I'll teach about four hours.

And Isobel has been asked to teach small children at the Bombay Scottish school, and she's also been asked to help with the pavement Club in Colaba where they take children who live on the sidewalks, and bath them, and feed them, and teach them songs about Jesus, and some bible stories.

Our third letter from Bombay.

Isobel and I are always thrilled when God opens unto us a door of utterance, to speak the mystery of Christ.

October 10th was a special day. God allowed us to minister to two people, both demonically cursed through witchcraft. Midmorning Isobel and I intended to go shopping together, but I was enjoying a special prayer session with the Lord, and I said I'd join her in half an hour. She left.

Soon after Isobel left, a man came to our door, and said that Pastor Joseph had sent him to me. The phones seldom work in India, so it was possible that Pastor Joseph had tried to phone me. We don't actually have a phone, but the owner of the building (the lawyer and his parents) have a phone upstairs, and they send their servant to get us, when it rings for us. This man whose name is Ramesh, had considerable trouble trying to define his problem, but after some prayer, he told me how his Hindu parents are constantly paying a witch doctor, to put curses on him. And for more than a year now, since no one at the church has been able to help him, he regularly pays the same witch doctor, to take the curses off of him. And it has kept him and his wife broke, and he has spent most of his time in terrible pain.

He gets stomach cramps, which only the witch doctor can remove.

Well, I prayed, and God showed me clearly that Ramesh had never been taught to defend himself. First I cast all the demons out of him. Then I laid hands on him to receive the Holy Spirit. Then I taught him about the power of tongues and laid hands on him to receive tongues. Then I taught him to resist the devil in Jesus name and in tongues.

I've seen him since then and he has no further trouble.

In the afternoon, we were invited to the "Little Sisters" "home for the aged". This is a very well run old folks home, and the nuns were very gracious to us all afternoon and evening.

We prayed for many, and we were blessed.

And one lady named Julie Pinto had the same trouble, exactly like Ramesh. Because she had become a Christian, some people used witchcraft, to cripple her, and give her terrible stomach pains. Evidently in both cases, these witchdoctors use potions, made of animal blood, and leaves, and a few other things. It was obviously real, and working, but I used Jesus name to cast those evil spirits out, and Julie was set free of all pain, confusion, and sickness. Then I taught her to defend herself. In both cases, I wrote all the instructions out for them, so they couldn't forget. Since then I've done some enquiring, and sending curses by witchcraft, seems to be very common here.

We have a number of riots here, mostly due to strikes. The millworkers, the police, the civil servants, the doctors, the high school students, the bus drivers, the universities, all on strike for various reasons.

Our trains are always overcrowded. People hang from the windows outside, and from the doorways and they stand on the roof. And the trains travel fifty miles per hour and because of the tracks, it seems like a hundred. The panic at all stations, of people trying to get on, is really something to experience. And at rush hours it 's incredible. People take a taxi to a less busy station up the line, to catch an incoming train, to be able to get on the outgoing train home. From 7:00 am to 11:00 am and 4:00 pm to 9:00 pm there are seldom less than 10,000 people on the ramps and a train leaves every three minutes. About a dozen people are killed every day by trains. We've seen some. They take a makeshift stretcher, namely a set of poles with a cloth across it and pick up the body and carry it to the nearest police station. Sometimes they are still alive and apparently they cannot rush anyone to a hospital here, until an accident report has been made out by the police. All over India, if you take an accident victim of any kind to a hospital, they will refuse to do anything, until a local policeman has had a chance to make out his report. There are hundreds of strange and irritating stories, because of this law.

Isobel and I were near Church Gate Station when we noticed and elderly man laying in the gutter, off of the sidewalk. He was sick and terribly skinny and had only his not so white underwear on. We walked up to him and asked "do you speak English". He said, "yes". We said we would like to help him. Then he sat up and told us what had happened. His name was Jeffrey, and he had been a professor of English at the University of Cairo, in Egypt. He was from England.

His parents had both died and he was their only son.

When he retired, he decided to travel India. He loved Bombay, and as most tourists do, he drank the beer. The water isn't safe, so tourists drink the beer instead. Unfortunately, since Jeffrey really wasn't a drinker, he got drunk, and then he was robbed. They took everything. His passport, his money, his suitcase, his clothes that he was wearing, and his watch, and ring . They also took his credit cards. When he sobered up, he went to several government buildings, and told them his story. They always said the same thing. We have millions of people who have absolutely nothing, and we cannot help them either. He wanted a new passport, but without any identification papers, they could do nothing. It was several weeks later now, and he had not eaten, and was literally starving to death. We bought him groceries, and clothes, and found a room for him, and told him we would see him again soon. It seemed like every time we got to Church Gate Station, we would always find Jeffrey in some place. And we would always have time for him and bought him things.

We gave him our contact information in case he got into trouble again. The room we had found him, was owned by two ladies, who went out of their way to be kind to him. Jeffrey had an amazing gift of the English language, and always spoke so eloquently.

We tried to talk to Jeffrey about Jesus, every time we saw him, but he was hard to convince. He was set in his ways. We bought Jeffrey a very expensive English Bible, and he liked it. Jeffrey was entertaining.

He had some pretty amazing stories. One day a servant man came to us, and said Jeffrey was in the hospital, and they were going to cut off his leg. It was a long trip to the Hospital and when we got there, we enquired if we needed to pay for Jeffrey's treatment, however those two land ladies had paid for him.

Jeffrey was on the third floor. As is custom in India, when a person is in the hospital, the whole family moves in with that person, and they sleep on the floor and are there for the duration. No one needed to tell us where Jeffrey was. The moment we entered the ward, we could smell that Gangrene in his leg. He had a white sheet over his legs, and even with the medications, he had much pain. I asked to see his leg and it was horrible. I said to Jeffrey, "the only reason King Jesus let us find you that day, was for this moment, so that you could experience how real and great our God is. Would you like me to pray for your leg now?" and Jeffrey said "yes". I put my hands carefully on his leg and prayed. Nothing happened.

I prayed several times, and then I realized he was healed. I told him that even though there was no evidence of his healing, that he was healed. Then I told him that there was something that he must do, to receive his healing. I said, "Jeffrey, from now until I come back tomorrow,, you must continually thank King Jesus for your healing". If you fall asleep, that's alright, but as long as you're awake, just keep thanking him for your healing. Like a mantra.

Then we left.

The next day, we had our prayer meeting at the Pastors house, and we didn't get to the hospital until after lunch. There was Jeffrey, sitting on the bed, with his legs over the side, and grinning from ear to ear.

The doctor had come very early to cut off his leg, and then discovered that there was nothing wrong with him, and wrote him a note, dismissing him from the hospital. Jeffrey had asked the head nurse if he could stay until his preacher friend came back. I told Jeffrey that it was time to give his heart to Lord Jesus, and he said, "yes, I know." So we said a very nice sinners prayer together, and then I wrote him a small note, of how to get to a church I knew of, and that he needed now to get water baptized. He agreed, and we walked him back to where he lived. We never saw him again.

When King Jesus healed people and said," thy sins be forgiven thee", he also didn't see them again. It was like Jesus was saying to us, "your work with Jeffrey is finished."

Our water gets shut off for about 12 hours every day. But at least when we get water, it's got pressure and if we boil it, we can drink it. At Manmad, the water came on about half an hour a day. Even here in Bombay, many homes have terrible times with water. And millions of people have to buy water from trucks. It's still about 95 degrees in the daytime, and 88 to 90 at night. Your skin always feels oily.

I had a large lump under my arm, in my armpit.

And it was really sore. But I prayed and in a few hours it disappeared. It was a hard lump and at first I thought I had big trouble. And then I remembered my great big, wonderful God.

Shopping is very strange in India. One clerk is outside of the counter to sell to you. One behind the counter, is to explain things to you. Another is to take things off the shelf. Then, if you decide to buy, another might weigh it for you. Then another clerk will write up the bill. You then take the bill to another clerk, who is a cashier. Your bill gets used by an inventory clerk, and then you get your change. Then another clerk carries the merchandise from it's original place in the store to a wrapping desk. At this desk you present your paid and stamped bill, to finally get your goods. The lineups are wonderful too. That's your modern department store. That's why most people deal with the street vendors. The stores in front of the stores, on the sidewalks.

We try to be clever in all of our buying, but India is India. The corn is not yellow and is as hard as peanuts. Even canned corn. Until we found out where to buy chicken, our chickens were like leather. So stringy that it would end up like chewing gum. And it's against the law to kill young cows, so all their water buffalo live to a ripe old age, before they are slaughtered. We bought the best steaks possible when Isobel's friend came from Ireland, and none of us could bite through them. But they looked great.

Then the flour has these little white worms. So Isobel sifts the flour. And after the fourth sifting she is still getting these tiny worms in the sieve. But the boiling of the rice makes it all good. Our milk is quite strange too. There is a cream on the top of the bottle, so that when you peel off the tin foil lid, you can hold the bottle upside down and the solid cream holds the milk back from pouring. The cream looks like white wax. It's white, not yellow. They make a type of butter out of it, called gee.(pronounce the "g" like in gear).

I had written about an old lady who had been dying of cancer, and how she got healed. Well apparently she stayed healed right up until she died. I was called to come pray for the family. But some good came of it. The father is very close to becoming a Christian now. Strange how people can get healed and still die.

I've had it happen before. The pain leaves. They get stronger. Eat well. Look good. Full of joy. And die anyway. It happens. A couple of weeks ago a Catholic lady phoned to say her sister had just had an operation for a huge tumor in her head. But before the doctors could remove it, she had a massive heart attack and they just closed her up again. Would I go to the intensive care unit and pray. Of course I'd be glad to go. The whole family was there. Crying of course. I prayed over this bald unconscious lady. Then went back to the waiting area and assured the family that it was worth putting your complete trust in God. That our great God answers prayer. And two days later she died. And I was embarrassed. I've learned not to put God in a corner, but to allow room for God's decision.

Our place is one floor off the ground, and we have a very small balcony where we always eat our meals. And every night it is fascinating to watch the huge rats scurry around. A few weeks ago we watched some workmen close up two large sewer holes because someone had stolen the lids. They filled the holes with dirt and then the last eighteen inches was filled with bricks. These bricks were smashed solid with a heavy solid pipe, with a six inch square piece of half inch metal welded to the end. They took turns pounding these two holes solid. Then the last three inches was filled with concrete and troweled very nicely. That was at six o'clock. By nine o'clock the rats had dug beautiful big holes through both sewer openings about seven inches in diameter. We walked over to see them the next day and it's truly amazing.

The concrete is very hard and no one has bothered them since. The body part without the tail is at least 10 inches long. And at night they are everywhere in this city.

We had a super time at the Gideons retreat. Thanks for your prayers. God really blessed us, and they allowed me to teach for five hours. And I'm invited to another one in January. A three day national convention.

We just completed our campaign at Manmad. That trip started out a bit wild. Our train reservations got unreserved and so we took a taxi halfway. That Sikh Taxi driver took pride in his racing ability, and soon found four men in a new car to race him. They would both pass a vehicle at the same time with on coming traffic and frankly, we are still wondering how God saved us. We prayed that whole trip.

In Manmad, the beds and food was a bit rough, but the meetings were great. Isobel got dysentery the first day and spent every night on the toilet. Part of the problem was the toilet itself. Just a hole in the floor of the toilet room.

You get to appreciate why western toilets have water in them. The room had a strong odour. We assumed that all of the toilets fed into one pipe. No running water . Somehow I caught a bad cold. We prayed a lot, but it wasn't until we got back, that we got our cures. We had signs and wonders too. And some prophecy. Those people in Manmad need a church building, and a full time pastor. Joe Martin has been traveling back and forth every week for eighteen months, doing double duty. Nine hours by train each way. He's got another church in Bombay and a house group. I preached five times. You wouldn't believe the town itself. Seventy-six thousand people jammed together in such poor conditions. But they were very kind to us, and we love them.

We've had several meetings at two new house groups. One at Chembur and one at Goandi. My Friday night meeting in Matunga is still growing. And God has enlarged our work at the Bombay Scottish School. I now have a class following the general assembly. I've got all the graduating class, and I've been teaching them about life after death, and about our new covenant with God, and how to get salvation. They love to ask questions. Even such off subject questions like "what is Beirut really like".

Last night we were walking home late, when a truck came and almost killed us both, by pinning us against a metal fence. Isobel was still upset this morning. It was really frightening. It had to be an angel that saved us. This truck, with about six men in the cab and another ten in the back were laughing at how they almost killed us. And drove on. We told the police a few minutes later, but their only vehicle is a broken down old truck, that doesn't run any more. They said if we lodged a complaint, the best we could hope for in court, was that the driver would get a warning.

We don't have any dull days. We are always so busy. And we get very tired too.

Just before we went to Manmad, we had to put up with ten days of Hindu celebrating, where they play loud drums and music all night long. Yes, ten days of it. So many times I told Isobel "I wonder if they realize how blessed they are, that I am a Christian"

They held one of their dances right outside of our kitchen window with those big loudspeakers blaring all night and those awful drums. It gets very Satanic. We were exhausted before we started for Manmad. But we are back to normal now. Praise God.

Sometimes we wonder what it would be like to have a real glass of milk or a piece of lemon meringue pie. Often, I'll ask Isobel "what's for dinner honey" and she'll recite a menu that makes our mouths water and we both laugh.

When "Monsoon Season" arrives, it is announced by an intense period of heavy rain, booming thunder, and plenty of lightning. The monsoon rain starts in June and ends in September. This rain injects an amazing amount of vigor into people, and it's common to see children running about, dancing in the rain, and playing games. Even adults join in because it's so refreshing. Some areas in Calcutta had three to four feet of water, which doesn't drain away. Bombay usually had six to ten inches. And Monsoon time is always very hot and humid.

I bought this one as a rain hat. It unclips and folds down on the left side. 'Still have it in a box, in my garage.

The first year we found a place that made raincoats,

In a factory that had a four foot high ceiling. Everyone sitting on the floor sewing, and welding this vinyl plastic material into raincoats. Only one color. An army green. They custom made our two coats. Outside it was torrential rain. When we went outside with out new raincoats on, we began to sweat profusely, and we were soaking wet in the inside of our new coats. We soon came to the conclusion that we did not need these coats.

Because of all the junk in the water, and you cannot see what is on the ground, we always wear sandals in the water, in Monsoon time. And you walk around totally soaked through and through. We plastic bag the stuff inside our carry bags.

We're in the final stages of the "Applied Word Centre", and we are ready to start. We talked to a lot of churches, and we are expecting 200 students. We were held back with committees, at the Methodist Center and now we 've heard, that we'll get approval sometime this week. We hope to teach for 48 weeks.

This Sunday I'm preaching at Borivali. Next Sunday at Colaba and at Mahem. And on the 21st ,we are at the concluding session of a 10 day "Vacation Bible School" for approximately 200 teenagers. Their theme is "bearing fruit for Jesus". That's in a small town called Kalyan. We'll go by train again.

On Thursday a lady phoned from Colaba to tell me that she is a friend of a lady I had prayed for. The lady I had prayed for, was completely healed now of stomach cancer and all pain was gone too. I said to her, "I wish God would do these things while I am there". She said, "well my friend is healed because you prayed". And then she added, "would you please come and pray for me." I said, "sure, when".

And we arranged to meet Saturday. Well, she didn't tell me on the phone what was wrong, which was also a bit exciting.

But after some trouble and much walking, I managed to find her in Colaba, which is about twenty five miles from where we live, and she is a lovely sixty five year old Catholic lady, who had arthritis and a lot of other things. This huge woman could hardly walk. She had a swollen stomach; swollen legs and she had faith. And she got instantly healed. Then she asked if I'd pray for her niece who had asthma. She got instantly healed too. Her niece's husband had chest pains and had had a heart attack, even though he looked just over thirty. And he was healed.

Then three girls who also live there, all in their twenties had "stomach pains", another "fever and pain" and another "dysentery and no energy and pains". All were cured instantly. Finally a waiter who had ulcers was also healed. And then I preached. Many people had gathered, and I knew it was of God. I told them, it was one thing to get healed and another thing to keep a healing. The spirit of sickness comes back, and needs to be rejected, and cast away, again and again, until it doesn't return. The Bible says if we resist the devil, he will flee from us. James 4:7

But if we don't resist, he won't flee. Jesus has given his disciples power against unclean spirits, to cast them out, and to heal all manner of sickness, and all manner of disease. (St. Matthew 10:1)

He has told us to preach and heal the sick. (St. Matthew 10: 7 - 8)

But we have no power to do this on our own.

The devil is not afraid of us.

No matter how much we yell at him, sickness and pain won't leave, until we use that Holy name of "Jesus". The only thing the devil is afraid of, is Jesus. Jesus told us in St. Matthew 28 : 18 "All power is given unto me, in heaven and in earth".

And when King Jesus sent out his seventy disciples, (35 pairs) to heal the sick and preach the Kingdom of God (St. Luke 10 : 9) they did it and came back with joy saying "even the devils are subject unto us, through thy name. (St. Luke 10 : 17)

That is the secret.

That is the power, that you can resist the devil with.

So when any kind of trouble comes back to you, resist by saying "get away from me trouble, in the name of Jesus".

Or, "in the name of Jesus, pain get out of me now.

I am healed by the stripes of Jesus". (1 Peter 2 : 24)

There is always a choice to be made.

When pain returns, it is very real. You can murmur (as people did in Numbers 11:1 or you can praise Jesus and resist the devil.) That is why he said: there hath no temptation taken you, but such as is common to man.

But God is faithful, who will not suffer you to be tempted above that ye are able.

But will, with the temptation also make a way to escape, that ye may be able to bear it. (1 Corinthians 10 : 13)

So our choice, when pain returns, is to murmur or resist in "Jesus" name. And then of course there is the timing of God. I tell people they are healed, even when they so obviously are not. I tell them that you just can't see it yet, but you are. Believe it.

Praise God for it and wait. Just praise him. Nothing else. I really wish God would work with me every time like he did on Saturday, but he doesn't. And sometimes, I get to hear about the healing weeks later, and it encourages me to go on. (I just do my part and he does his. Don't be tempted to murmur. He won't break his word. We know who the enemy is.

I should add something here. Some of you are wondering if I, just at random declare a person healed. That's not true. I operate in the spirit and God shows me when I can stop praying and tell the person that they are healed. Sometimes God just tells me to stop praying but doesn't tell me they are healed.

Jesus went about doing good and healing all that were oppressed of the devil. The devil attacks Christians as much as we let him. And Jesus said: "behold, I give you power to tread on serpents and scorpions and over all the power of the enemy, and nothing shall by any means hurt you. (St Luke 10 : 19)

My Barber is a Moslem. A skinny man who tries extremely hard to be pleasant. I told him that I teach people about Jesus, and I pray for the sick, and Jesus heals them. "Really, Jesus heals them?" "Really".

"Can he heal my son?" "Yes, when can I come to your house?" We arranged for Thursday.

His son was retarded. He is not now. Also the barber himself had a severe case of arthritis, which I really had not noticed. His hips and legs were in terrible pain. That left instantly. You should have seen him cry. With joy of course. Me too.

And then I prayed for half the neighbor hood. But not before preaching. Told them all about Jesus. And salvation.

The day before, God told me to buy a Bible for my Barber. And I bought an Urdu Bible for him. Not a cheap one either.

But while I was there in the Bible store, which was more than twenty miles from where we live, I was in the spirit, and God told me to buy an Arabic Bible, and I didn't see why, so I didn't get it, because it was also expensive. I disobeyed.

It turned out that Qamar, my Barber, has a sister who is educated, and reads only Arabic. Moslem girls learn Arabic, to read the Quran. She herself has a hole in her throat to breathe, and talk. She really was keen to learn more about the healing person, Jesus.

All teaching at Qamar's house had to be interpreted by him in Urdu.

That's usually the way it is here. But God always gives me an interpreter. Now I'm going back next Thursday on Qumar's day off, to bring the Arabic Bible and to teach again.

God keeps opening doors for me.

An Oil Company manager sat down at the only empty chair in the restaurant, right beside Isobel and I. we both knew it was of the Lord.

We told him so. There must be a reason why God sent you to us. A few minutes earlier, he had been upstairs in his room considering going up to the roof to jump off.

Yes, suicide.!

He was a wreck. He knew all about Jesus from the Full Gospel Businessmen. But he had backslidden.

It was God's timing.

We lead him back to Jesus. We've bought him a very good Bible, he's been to church and two Bible studies with us, and he's a new man. He had given up when he got a telegram, that his wife wanted a divorce. The poor man didn't know which way to turn, and God led him to us. We've asked God to work mightily in his wife 's life too. She'll come back to him now. Because God answers prayer.

Thousands of kids are flying kites in Bombay at this time of year, because of the wind, after the monsoons. And the trick seems to be, to get the kite flying as high and as far away as possible. To do this, very good nylon string has to be used.

A friend of ours came to a bible study two weeks ago and told us of how his neighbor had been riding his motor scooter, and a kite went down and the string cut his neck and killed him instantly.

The week before that, we were to get a terrible cyclone here in Bombay, and everyone was preparing for it, and it was quite terrifying. Everything was so quiet. No birds or animals. Very few people. High wind, dark clouds moving about so fast. And because of our Tonga experience, I knew what had to be done. We prayed for two days, and God turned the storm, and it hit north of Bombay. Still about five hundred people died, but millions would have died in Bombay.

Following the cyclone, the Hindu's had their "Duvale". It is pronounced "Do Valley". It is their New Year.

For ten days and more, it was like a war zone in Bombay. Firecrackers, which make a four storey building quiver and things jump in your house.

And they hurt our ears so much, that we wore earphones and pillows at night to get away from it. We can really sympathize with the Lebanese. We only had ten days of it. For three days they went off all night, but before that, they quit about 1:00 am.

And they would start again when the sun came up. They even threw a huge bomb right into our living room but miraculously, nothing was damaged, and we just praise God for guarding us like that.

We had a great time in Kalyan.

Lovely train ride there.

They had a church parade around the city.

Then they sang in many groups and finally I preached. Then they put on a series of plays and were really very good. And last of all we were honored with handing out the prizes for the outstanding students, in all the classes, and events. We did make one mistake.

They brought us some sweetened colored water, which they were giving all the children, and it would have been rude to refuse. We prayed over it, but for the next few days, we really suffered. I got over it faster, but after three days Isobel's pain became unbearable, and she was rushed to a doctor, where she received an injection, and within two days she was cured. We prayed a lot during those hours.

And King Jesus healed us. We didn't die.

But people actually do die of dysentery and diarrhea.

According to the Express magazine here in Bombay, last year, at least one and a half million deaths in India, were caused by diarrhea diseases.

Every third Indian man, woman and child is attacked by diarrhea and dysentery at least once a year.

The same article also reported :
40 million – suffer from Goitre, which arises from iodine deficiency
68 million - handicapped - 10 % of the population
15 million - blind and 50,000 children go blind every year
4 million - lepers, of which 3 ½ million have been patients but only about 200,000 get treated.
15 million - tuberculosis
15 million - diseases as children, which make them unemployable if they survive.
100 million - filaria and malaria and dengue fevers.

If you read Deuteronomy 28:1-62
You see why this is so, and verses 61 and 62 define their destiny. Most of India are idol worshippers, and in Exodus 23 : 24 -25 God tells us why they have the diseases, and how he will take the sickness away, from the midst of them.

We do a lot of witnessing. Last week alone we gave out thirty St. John's Gospel 's in Marathi, Hindi, and English. They are very cheap here and they also have a good salvation message in the back. Trains have become our main witnessing place because we have a captive audience for an hour each way. So we don't waste this time.

Isobel and I are out almost every night and seldom get home before eleven and often twelve midnight, and praise God, as he has guaranteed us in Psalms 91- and no evil has befallen us to date.

Although there are robberies and murders every night, and even as we are such obvious targets, being foreigners, God is greater. Hallelujah !

Thankyou Jesus .

"Christmas Eve" we spoiled ourselves and went to the Taj Mahal Hotel and had dinner in the Shamiana Room. (Shamiana means tent.)

You should go online, and look at how opulent the Taj Mahal Hotel is.

We had steak and peas, and it was delicious. After dinner we strolled in Colaba, behind the Taj Mahal (Colaba is a poor fishing village. Pastor John has a small church there.) As we were walking, we came upon a furniture store, and went inside, out of curiosity. We walked all around and came upon a picture of Moses on the mountain when he went up to get the 10 commandments.

It looks like God suddenly made lightening, and then Gods big voice said "Moses" and Moses flinches, and makes a fist, and in terror looks up at the lightning.

It's a large picture, and when we asked the price, it was far too high, so we walked out of the store.

A block away a young boy ran after us, and wanted us to return, as the store owner had reduced the price. It was still too high, so we walked out again.

Within a minute the boy came again and said the price would be good now. It was, and we bought it and it hangs in my office now.

I also used this picture for all four volumes of my books called "Questions to God."

We were looking forward to starting the school at the Methodist center. What we didn't realize, is that some pastors were against it. They thought we would steal their parishioners, and perhaps also start a church.

One pastor took it upon himself to meet with the Methodist Hierarchy and managed to convince them to cancel the project. They tactfully approached me to start a "business school" in the same center.

At this time our support finances were also strained.

Isobel and I determined that God was changing our direction, and we prepared to leave India.

I had to go to the Government office in Bombay to get the papers for our exit out of India, and when I left to walk back to the train station at Church Gate, I was attacked in broad daylight by four men. I managed to fight them off and ran to the train station. After I was on the train, a lady pointed to my leg and there was blood all around my shoe. I had been cut, but in the moment, I had not even noticed. When we got to Dadar, the lady offered to take me to her Doctor. It was a fair walk, and when we got there, she convinced the Doctor to take me in.

The odd thing about this Doctor was, that she was a gynecologist . She brought me into the office, and had me sit in that exam chair, with the stirrups for the feet. The cut was deep and long. She sewed up my leg and the lady who brought me there, paid for me. Again, God sent someone .

Our tickets were for London ,England.

A week later we took that "one hundred mile per hour" train through Wales to Holyhead, and then that huge ferry boat to Dublin, and stayed with Isobel's parents.

CHAPTER 27
Beautiful Ireland

Amazing missionary adventures

It was great to be with Isobel's parents. Loved the food. But the weather was something else. We couldn't get warm. India had thinned our blood.

When we left New Zealand, they gifted us each with those fishermen knit sweaters, which we now wore .

They didn't help much. We both got severe colds.

My leg wasn't healing, and it began to swell very large. It became very painful as well. Isobel got me to the Dublin Hospital, and they immediately serviced my leg.

They lanced it, and cleaned it out, and restitched it.

They gave me some antibiotics, and I went home.

Soon we were involved with Bible studies, and teaching sessions again. And some healings too.

Isobel's Catholic priest was very helpful in organizing places for me to go. Then someone suggested I go to "Trinity University" in Downtown Dublin, and they were very receptive. I ended up teaching there too.

Friends of Isobel's took us for a drive out in the country, and they showed us Glendalough Monastery, built in the sixth century by St. Kevin.

St. Kevin died in 618. The monastery lasted six centuries and survived the Vikings and the Normans but was finally destroyed by the English in 1398.

We also saw St. Kevin's stone church, which has a "stone roof", and a very nice "stone bell tower".

That's Isobel and Anne and Bren and their two kids.

Another day we went through Dublin Castle which was very impressive. A few days later, I flew to Vancouver, but Isobel wanted to stay a few more days with her parents. I went ahead to prepare a place for us to stay.

CHAPTER 28
Kelowna and Edmonton

Amazing missionary adventures

It was great to be back home again.

Isobel came home a few days later, and it was a different way of life.

My parents still had a weekly Bible study and soon I was embedded in weekly teaching. It was very enjoyable. I also got involved with their church.

It was amazing how busy I got, with both the church and with teaching. In June, Isobel got pregnant, and Sean was born in February. We were thrilled. We soon decided to move to Burnaby. I was also involved with the Full Gospel Businessmen.

I also made a few trips to Vancouver Island where I worked with several churches in Victoria, in Courtney, in Comox, in Nanaimo, in Black Creek, and in Port Alberni. I enjoyed teaching and people were healed. God kept me very busy. What was different this time, is that almost everyone that God sent to our meetings needed something. Many needed jobs. However most of the people who needed jobs, weren't really employable. Some had been in treatment homes, or recovery homes, or had disabilities, or had just not worked for a long time. But God is amazing. God only does wonderous things. (Psalms 72:18)

One lady got a job as a waitress. We could hardly believe it. A young man got a job as a truck driver delivering to grocery stores. That was also unbelievable. We always prayed for every one at every meeting. We would all hold all held hands. There was power in the room. We prayed in English, and then in tongues, and it worked. I would tell people, if you want your miracle to happen, start thanking him for it. Believe it in your heart.

King Jesus said, "thy faith hath made thee whole" (St. Matthew 9:22)

People always have someone in their life, who is a problem person. Sometimes it is another church member. Sometimes it is a person they work with. Sometimes it is a neighbour. Sometimes it is a relative or a family member. God knows exactly where he has placed you. And the people around you are your mission field. God is not going to send you out, until you start to work your missions field, where you are. I would tell my group, bring your problem person to our meetings. Tell them what goes on here and say that they need to see these things for themselves. These problem people have been placed in your "circle of influence", by God, for a purpose. You are their lifeline. You are on the wharf, and they are in the water, and they don't even know that they are drowning. You can have apathy toward your problem person, or you can have empathy for their soul. If you are a soul winner, God will work with you.

If you are a consistent soul winner, God, who watches everything you do, and everything you say, will broaden your mission field. (St. Matthew 12: 36-37)

And that's how you enter servant mode and become a missionary.

Many potential missionaries make the mistake of hoping their local church will allow them to be recognized and let them do the occasional preaching.

What these potential missionaries need to know, is that the local pastors consider such a person trouble, and believe that if they help this person, he will become a threat to start his own church, by taking away some of their congregation.

The work on Vancouver Island went very well, and in many places people received the Baptism of the Holy Spirit. This would follow with the gifts of the Holy Spirit . (1 Corinthians 12: 7-11)

God allowed me to be in the Spirit with a Spirit of Discernment, and a Spirit of knowledge to see what gifts the Holy Spirit had given to this congregation. It was interesting to see to whom God gave the gifts. A young boy about 13 got the gift of healing and immediately we experimented by him laying hands on someone who needed healing, and it worked. Then he laid hands on others, and the Holy Spirit confirmed his gift.

An elderly woman received the gift of prophecy, and she also was proficient in that gift.

It was like that in several congregations.

Some weeks later, in May, Isobel became pregnant, and we began making new plans. We wanted to be on our own, so we moved out of my parents house in Kelowna, into a one bedroom apartment in the same area. We had one chair, no table. A mattress on the floor. Just a few clothes. We ate at the kitchen counter standing up. And we were very happy.

Gradually, we got a few extras like dishes. We also began to make plans for leaving Kelowna. We knew that I needed to do more. And I needed to support my wife. Sean was born in February, and I almost lost Isobel in the birth. It was very close. But God helped us again. And Sean was perfect. Isobel recovered.

In fall I made a trip across Canada and preached in many churches. One of them was a church in North Bay, Ontario. I worked with this church for a while, and they liked me. I also preached in Sioux St. Marie, Winnipeg, and in Edmonton . I worked with the church in Winnipeg for a week, And a church in Edmonton. Also a group outside of Edmonton, in Sherbrook Park. Then Max Solbrechen invited me to preach in his church. It was arranged to start on Sunday morning.

A teacher from Sherwood Park, a suburb of Edmonton, had lent me a small red car, and I drove to a church group east of Edmonton. It was snowing from the time I started, and it became quite precarious. I was still in Edmonton city, and cars were sliding around, and I said to God, why did you send me here, in this dangerous place.

And suddenly God gave me a song :
" my yoke is easy,
and my burden is light,
my yoke is easy
and my burden is light ,
if you're doing it the hard way,
who do you think that's from;
my yoke is easy,
and my burden is light."

I began to rebuke the demons around me .
Then I prayed for God to get me through safely.
He did. All the way east, I did not have a bit of trouble.

The meeting I went to, lasted well after midnight, when suddenly, I had terrible stomach pains.

They prayed for me, and I left. It was already Saturday. I was still hoping to do tomorrows "Sunday service", in Max's Church. But I wasn't sure I'd make it. It was about a hundred mile trip. I had terrible pains. I actually don't remember most of the trip. Suddenly I was in the parking lot of the Edmonton General Hospital. I didn't have that address, and I still have to assume that angels drove me there. Somehow, I went into the emergency, and I must have passed out. When I awoke, I had terrible pain and they told me, that they had taken my gall bladder out. I had an eleven inch diagonal cut across my stomach. Within two hours, the nursing staff wanted me to walk around the hallways. I could barely stand up. I met other people in the waiting room down the hall, and I expressed that I had horrible pain, but that when I asked for pain killers, the staff said that I had just had the pain injection, and that I would have to wait several hours. They all had the same story.

Then one girl said they had given her morphine, but that couldn't be true, because she was very allergic to morphine. We all began to compare notes and soon found out that none of us had actually received any form of pain injections before or after the operations. I went to a pay phone and dialed 911 and asked for the RCMP. They came to the Hospital to interview us, and then interviewed all the Doctors and the nurses, and then arrested about twenty of them. It made front page of the Edmonton newspaper the next morning. Meanwhile the man whose car I had been driving, phoned that place east of Edmonton and found out that I had terrible stomach pains, and since I didn't return his car, he phoned the hospital on Saturday morning, and then came to see me. I asked him to call Max Solbrechen and cancel.

He was most kind to me and was amazed at what had happened at the hospital. That staff had a large drug business and were now out of business. God still has complete control.

My parents drove to Edmonton from Kelowna, in their motor home, to take me home. I had already booked many places on Vancouver Island and the following Saturday; I started meetings in Courtenay.

Yes, my stomach was still sore. The Doctor had used large staples to sew up my eleven inch cut, and they were not taken out yet. Years later my stomach bulged out of that cut, and a Doctor Joyce sewed a synthetic netting underneath it, to keep it flat. It's still flat.

One day I got a call from a pastor, to go to pray with someone in the Burnaby General Hospital. I asked who is it, and he said, "Rev. Frank Pace". I told him that I knew Frank and would be glad to go. I went that same day. Frank was in the ICU unit, under critical care. The nurses told me that I could not go in. I explained that I needed to go in to pray. It would save his life. They were shocked that I was that bold. The minute I went into ICU, I knew what was wrong.

I knew that smell from India. Jeffrey had the same smell. I greeted Frank, and he remembered me. He said they were going to cut it off at the knee. I said , "no they won't, King Jesus is still doing healings".

I put my hands on his leg and began to pray. From the moment I started, it was as if King Jesus had just entered the room. Both of us could feel the anointing.

I could also feel the heat in my hands. Frank said, "I can feel it." I said, "so can I" Frank cried and so did I.

Then we both began to praise the Lord. The nurses outside could hear it. Eventually we stopped and pulled back the sheet and nothing much had changed.

I told Frank he was healed. He said, "I believe it".

Before I left, I told Frank the same thing I told Jeffrey.

"Keep on thanking the Lord" for as long as you can. It's OK if you fall asleep but thank him for healing you.

I'll be back tomorrow. I did come back. I cannot remember what delayed me, but when I came back Frank was gone. The Nurses assured me that Frank had gone home, and that he did not get his leg cut off.

I have never seen Frank again. Months later someone said that Frank had gone back home to the USA.

CHAPTER 29
Vancouver Island

Amazing missionary adventures

My brother Stan went to Courtenay, ahead of me to pray. The first night (on Saturday) the Full Gospel Businessmen, had arranged for me to do a very large banquet, at the Holiday Inn in Courtenay, which would include most of the chapters on the Island. About three hundred people. I had previously worked with five churches in the area:

Christ Church Cathedral- Pastor Charles Dorrington

The United Church -with Pastor Ray Brandon

The Pentecostal Church – with Pastor Ros Fox

The Catholic Church - with a Priest

The Black Creek Church -Pastor Evaldo Filiponi

Some of their people came too.

Stan was there a day early and spent the entire day praying over every chair, for the people that would attend. I had nothing to do with that, and did not even know that Stan would be there.

The banquet went well, and when all the preliminaries were done, I was asked to start.

I have a habit at all of my meetings, to start by raising my hands above my head, and praying in English and then in tongues, and I never rush this part. The Lord showed me to pray for the Holy Spirit to fall on us. I prayed that .

Suddenly, the entire audience fell to the ground. Everyone. You should have seen it. It was really amazing. It took quite a long time. No one was hurt. Many were speaking in tongues. Many were healed. Most were crying. The Holy Spirit had touched everyone. People were changed.

I had planned to give my testimony. But now it was redundant. Instead I taught about the Holy Spirit, concerning the Spiritual Gifts. (1 Corinthians 12 : 1-11)

What is usually left out in this teaching, is how it actually works in a church.

Also who has the gifts, and will they be used and how.

The United Church, downtown in Courtenay was a real joy to work with. The entire Church was ready to learn. Being in learning mode, is so much easier, than teaching people who are sitting there, criticizing, and comparing every precept, to what they already know.

I had a second meeting with a Group in Port Alberni, and was pleasantly surprised, when, before I got up to speak, several people came to the front and testified how they had received healings, the last time I was there. The healings evidently did not happen instantly like I always hope they should.

But then the same group didn't like what I taught later, because it wasn't the same as what they had been taught. This has happened to me many times around the world. People prefer to learn things that they have been taught by there eldership.

They are not prepared to change. King Jesus had the same problem. So did St. Paul.

Charles Dorrington , the Pastor of the Anglican Church beside the Empress Hotel in Victoria, was very kind to invite me to hold teaching meetings several times.

When I got saved in Anaheim, California, the next morning, the main speaker was Doctor Doug Roberts of Victoria, B.C.

Doug had written a great book called "To Adam with Love". He spoke to the audience (about twenty five thousand people) about marriage.

Now, years later, I was asked to come to Victoria, to pray for Doctor Doug Roberts. He had brain cancer and a tumor, and a large group were going to gather in a community hall to pray with Doug.

I went and got to lay hands on his head, and prayed, and the Lord showed me that the tumor would come out, and Dr. Roberts would be healed. I was notified a couple of weeks later that Doctor Roberts had been operated on, and the tumor had just rolled out, as if it had been already operated on by someone else. I recalled the young boy at Avis and Johnny's house in Kalina (Bombay) . Same thing.

Within a few weeks, Dr. Roberts arranged an all day teaching session for me, in Victoria, at a Hotel Conference Room, and about fifty men showed up.

A couple of years later, Dr. Doug Roberts brother in law, Brian Ruud started a church in Victoria, and my brother Roy and his wife attended, and got saved. Brian also baptized them both, in a swimming pool. Brian Rudd had been in Australia and New Zealand holding stadium meetings, with great success. One of the things I had noted, was that at these stadiums, Brian had been teaching out of The Acts 19: 18 -20, and thousands of people brought their T.V.'s, books, records, etc., and made a huge bonfire in the middle of the stadium grounds and burned them before the Lord.

I also loved Brian's teaching on Psalms chapter 1.

You can see it on YouTube.

CHAPTER 30
Burnaby and Surrey

Amazing missionary adventures

We moved from Kelowna to Burnaby to an Apartment on the 14th floor (actually it was the thirteenth floor, but because of superstition, they had numbered it fourteen) It was right beside Lougheed Mall on the west side. It was very convenient. To support my family, I prayed again for direction, and God decided to have me drive taxi again, which gave me a certain amount of flexibility for ministry. I drove for MacLure's Cabs at Granville Island in Vancouver.

Within a couple of months, the owners at MacLure's Cabs asked me to become the manager. After about a year, another man wanted to be the manager, and I was asked to resign.

Within a week, I was asked to be the manager of Vancouver Taxi, which was a bigger company.

The Lord had again closed a door and opened another door. And the pay was higher too.

I managed Vancouver Taxi for a couple of years and then one day, two of their owners asked me to do something special. Both of them were on workers compensation, because of separate car accident injuries, but both of them were still working as drivers as well. They wanted me to change the paperwork, so that it would be recorded that someone else was driving their cars, so that they could continue to receive the benefits of compensation. I refused to do it, and the next day the board of directors fired me.

I thought of doing many things, but the Lord assured me that he would take care of me, as he always had.

And he would also take care of the men, who wanted me to commit fraud.

Isobel and I prayed and asked the Lord what I should do now, and we determined that I should go back to India to Bombay, for three months. I was immediately immersed in teaching again. I really missed Isobel and my son Sean. But I kept very busy, and the Lord worked with me in the meetings. People were saved and many were healed. It was as if I had never left Bombay.

The three months went quickly and finally, it was great to be back again. I was soon hired as the manager of Yellow Cabs (the largest Taxi company in Vancouver, with four hundred and eighty cabs) and the money was great too. The job was challenging, but I loved it.

One day I met a couple of Vancouver Taxi owners and asked them how it turned out for the owners who wanted me to change their trip sheets. They said, "You don't know?" I said, "no". Turned out, the one owner, who was about thirty five years old and an extremely good soccer player, had determined to go back to Ludhiana in Punjab to avoid incrimination.

At the Airport in Vancouver, at the inspection customs counter, he suffered a major heart attack and died on the conveyer belt, just before the xray machine.

And the other man, the same week, had his taxi in the garage, and was getting something out of the trunk, when another (new) driver drove into the yard, to go to the garage, and was somehow distracted, and accidently stepped on the gas peddle, instead of the brake peddle, and smashed into the car parked in the garage. The driver who was bent over the trunk, had his lower body crushed so badly, that he is permanently in a wheelchair, and had many operations. (Hebrews 10: 30 -31)

Our apartment on the fourteenth floor had a small balcony. One day Sean had climbed through the open balcony door and was holding on to the railing. It horrified Isobel, and we decided to move to Surrey, to a townhouse. We had a new lifestyle. But it was a long way to go to work, and the Lord helped in changing that too.

I got a job managing Surdel Taxi, and the office was about two miles away. After about two years, I had to fire an owner, who had been drinking while driving and had also molested a female passenger, who had phoned me with her complaint. The president asked me to squash the complaint and I refused. I was fired.

Within a couple of weeks I became the manager of Pacific Cabs, which serviced Langley and Aldergrove.

It was a good job, and it was easy for me. Two months later, the President of Surdel Taxi, who had fired me, (he was about 50 years old) died of a heart attack at home. I actually really liked the man.

I went to his funeral. No one said anything. All of the taxi industry was there, from all of the other companies in Vancouver too. They all knew, but no one said anything. Everyone had for years known that I was a missionary, and I had talked Christianity to most of them. Everyone greeted me with much respect.

CHAPTER 31
North Bay Ontario

Amazing missionary adventures

One day we received a call from North Bay, Ontario to pastor a church there. When I had been there, it was a good church, with around two hundred people. But now it had shrunk to just a few families, and they needed me to work there. Isobel and I prayed about it and took a train to North Bay. Sean was two and loved the train. The train rattled terribly all the way, like it had a thousand loose rivets. But we were more concerned about what we were heading into.

Pastoring is hard work. Everyone wants attention.

The church was in disarray. Both the people, and the physical building. The roof had caved in on this beautiful old brick church. Probably because of snow. The church also had a steeple, but no bell. All of our services were in the basement. Because of the small congregation, the roof was not on the agenda. I worked hard at being a good pastor.

To increase the income, we decided to start a daycare. I bought children's tables and chairs.

There was a good kitchen, but we bought things for children. Several mothers volunteered to run the daycare. We had it all set up perfectly and then we advertised in the local paper. Our location was good, and our staff was good. The setting with play equipment and climbing equipment was first class.

What no one in the church knew, including me, is that you must have educated staff, to look after children.

A two year course called "Early Childhood Education" was mandatory. The only one in North Bay who had this degree, was a lady competitor.

We would also need a "Professional Day Care Owner Certificate". Another 8 week course. The project ended there. Not one of us knew babysitting was this complicated.

Isobel was pregnant again and winter in North Bay is awesome. You can shovel the driveway, and two hours later you've got another two feet of snow. The snow beside the driveway was about seven feet high.

Sometimes we would open the front door, and the snow was higher than the door frame. David was born in February and our family was beautiful.

We lasted just over a year. We built the church up to over two hundred people again, and then the former pastor wanted the church back, and Isobel was more than ready to go back to Surrey.

CHAPTER 32
Back in Surrey

Amazing missionary adventures

I was still doing Bible studies and Full Gospel Businessmen's Banquets, in many places.

And I was now driving Taxi at Yellow Cabs.

I fellow had heard me speak at a banquet, and invited me to lunch, and asked me, if I knew anything about sales and marketing. He had a two year old company and needed help promoting his machinery. I had a strong business acumen from Toronto and fit into the marketing and sales of this company well. He offered me a job, and I left the Taxi business to join a machinery manufacturing company. Our marketing included huge magazine advertising, and we also did trade shows. Some years, I did forty-two shows a year. Eventually I became a Vice president and was in charge of all the dealers in North America including Canada, U.S.A., and Mexico. The company grew and it was eventually sold to a group from Singapore. And it is still amazing, how much ministry the Lord has given me in this job.

I also found out, that working a booth in a show, was also great opportunity, and God brought me the right people. The more I talked about God, the better my sales were. God is the blesser. When our son's got older, Isobel came to some of the shows with me. Because I traveled so much, I got first class privilege on the aircraft, and it was great.

One time, we went to the SEMA show in Las Vegas, and after the show, we were walking in front of the Bellagio Hotel, and in front of us was a family.

A husband and wife and three small children. Girls about nine and seven and a boy about five. The little boy was limping and when I looked, he was wearing the thongs, with that strap thing beside the big toe, but the thongs were worn out, and the right one was too short for his foot. So he was walking on skin, and it was starting to bleed. I looked at Isobel and said, "we're buying shoes" She nodded. I walked up to the father and said," would it be alright, if my wife and I bought your family shoes?" He looked at me and wondered if I was a problem, or if he had heard right.

After a moment he nodded, sure. There are no shoe stores near the Bellagio, so we had to walk all the way back to Sands Ave. just passed the Treasure Island Hotel. The mall on the other side has a shoe store on the third floor. I carried the boy some of the way. We bought the three children those runners, that have those lights in them. And bags of socks. Isobel and the mother helped put them on. Then the kids all began to jump around with glee. You should have heard them squealing with joy. It was awesome. We also bought the parents really good shoes and bags of socks. They were both crying, and then the husband explained that they were from Kansas, and had driven their Volkswagen van to Vegas, because they had heard it was easy to get a job here. But they were very dirty. They had to park outside of the city limits and were beside a ditch, where they could wash up. They had run out of money a few days ago, but you cannot beg in Las Vegas, so they were all very hungry. I pulled out several hundred dollars and gave it to them. (Deuteronomy 15:7-11) We never did exchange names.

When I teach, I stress that God always wants us to give. He rewards those that give.

Jesus said, "it is better to give than to receive". Why better? Because God rewards. Then the question is, who do you give to? Why trust someone else with your money, hoping that they will give it to someone needy. Always carry with you, what you can afford to give. Then, when God shows you someone to give to, you have it with you, immediately to give. Some can give much, and some can give a little. But have it ready.

I was in a grocery store and our basket was more than full. And the lady behind us had two children and had one quart of milk and a package of wieners, and a loaf of bread. Anyone could see that she was in trouble. I handed her all the money I had in my pocket and said go buy the rest of it. She cried and left. When she was gone, I cried too. Grateful that God had let me see that.

One time I was on a plane from Kansas City to Miami. The lady beside me was very friendly and wanted to tell me about her son. His name was Zack and so I asked her if she had named him after the prophet in the Bible. She said yes, Zechariah, but her son preferred to be called just "Zack". I asked, "what does he do?" And she proudly said, "tomorrow he is starting his first professional golf game with the PGA."

I said , "I'm a golfer, and love to watch golf on T.V.

What's your last name?" She said, "Johnson"

At this time I knew nothing about Zack Johnson, but I asked her if I could pray for God to bless him. At this point several people had begun to listen in. So I prayed loud enough for everyone to hear. She immediately asked me about my Christianity, and I told her. Then I asked if she would like to hear of some of my missionary experiences. The Lord had opened a door. For over an hour I had a captive audience and probably twenty people listening. I prayed for some others at the end.

Since then, I've concluded that "plane time" is also of the Lord.

So I've prayed for it, and God consistently opens doors.

I was on a plane more that twice a week. Most of my flights had connections, so that I was on a plane about four times a week.

I also began to write. Mostly a Bible study course.

'Thought that people might take this course and teach, without me being there.

Then the Lord changed my course and told me to write books. He said he would give me the words. And the finances. And the time to write.

I was retiring. Sixty five years old. They gave me gifts.

My best gift was a very expensive Scotty Cameron putter.

I was retired and loved golf. "Guildford Golf Course" offered me the job of "Marshall". Start at 6:00 am and sand the "par three tee's". Work until two o'clock. Only two days a week, ten dollars an hour. And any time I wanted, I could bring three friends and golf for free.

I thought I had it made. I didn't need the money, but this was great. On the third day, I was on the seventeenth tee, which was elevated about four feet and had steps to it. I was finished sanding and took a short cut and walked down the grass slope instead of taking the steps, slid down the slope, dropped the sand box, my hat went flying, I got all wet from the dew, and I broke my leg, broke my ankle, and broke my foot. The cart was about twenty feet away. The club house was a mile away. There was no one on the course. I got very dirty crawling to the cart. Managed to grab my new "Taylor Made" hat on the way and crawled up the cart.

I was in huge pain. I drove with my left leg all the way back and every bump was super painful. When I parked in front of the club house, I waved at the young girl at the counter inside, and frantically tried to get her to come outside. She just waved back.

Then I phoned my wife who was still sleeping. She was a good thirty minutes away, but she did come and drove me to the hospital. In the hospital I asked for pain killers. I was on a terrible mobile bed, in a hallway, and they said, "not until the Doctor comes to see me."

It took eleven hours, before the Doctor came, and he did order pain killers, and an hour later he operated on my leg. I still have two bolts in my ankle.

But what was amazing, is that I now was confined to sitting for the next seven months. I started to write, and I finished Volume one during that time. The Lord taught me to write his way. The whole accident was so that I would take the time to write.

I've been writing ever since. I've now finished five books. 'Currently have three more started.

CHAPTER 33
Promontory, Chilliwack, B.C.

Amazing missionary adventures

For the last two years, I walk our little dog "Marley" (a female, half beagle, and half King Charles) every day to my "prayer bench". It's at the top of a mountain on a nice trail. The prayer bench has an incredible view of a river at the very bottom (about two thousand feet down) and a lake about two miles on the other side of the River. There are taller mountains on the other side. Isobel and I both love the walk. In summer there are rabbits everywhere, and squirrels. (and eagles and brown bears)

But almost every day God brings me a new person to talk to about Jesus. I sit praying, on my prayer bench, and sure enough, God brings someone to me. I usually get at least half an hour to talk. Sometimes more. I talk to people everywhere I go about Jesus, and I usually get to pray with them. There are no coincidences. God prepares them, and most of the time it's obvious that they were sent. Sometimes it's a father with two twenty year old sons. Sometimes a mother and a daughter. Sometimes it's an older man that has just lost his wife. Sometimes it is three ladies that have been friends for years. It's always God.

Today, it was a man about forty, who said he was not a Christian, but had been to Sunday School when he was young. His parents had also not been Christians.

We spent over an hour together. He will study my first book on e-book. He knows now that he must make a decision. Not making a decision is also a decision.

Please pray for Isobel and I. I had cancer from August 2021 to March 2022. The tumor is gone too.

(30 chemo and 30 radiation treatments)

The doctors and all the CT scans and MRI's say, I have no cancer in my body now.

We hope to get back on the road again soon.

I have also started three more books.

You can write to me at :
ronaldfpeters@gmail.com

I will answer all of my emails.

Buying the Books

Friesen Press has published the first five books.

Questions to God , By Ronald F. Peters
Volume 1, The Mystery of Life After Death

Questions to God, By Ronald F. Peters
Volume 2, The Actual Doctrine Of King Jesus

Questions to God, By Ronald F. Peters
Volume 3, My Sheep Hear my Voice

Question To God, By Ronald F. Peters
Volume 4, Messed up Families

Amazing missionary adventures, By Ronald F. Peters
Volume 5, (what is it like to be a missionary)

God's plan for churches, by Ronald F. Peters
Volume 6 - It starts with a teachable spirit

Order the books from "Friesen Press bookstore"

You can also order the books (hardcover and paperback and e-books) through the other Online distributors.

Amazon Kindle Store
Ingram Book Store
Kobo Store
Nook Store
Google Play
Apple Books

Questions
(to God)

Ronald F. Peters

VOLUME 1: The Mystery of Life after Death

"The Mystery of Life after Death"

Ron's office

Ron and Isobel

The air up here is so nice.
And the presence of God is so overwhelming

The view from the prayer bench

Marley in prayer mode

Printed in the USA
CPSIA information can be obtained
at www.ICGtesting.com
JSHW022108060823
46004JS00001B/7